KMC
irklees

AF470590

232 3452 02

Sharron Davies

AGAINST THE TIDE

Sharron Davies

AGAINST THE TIDE

WILLOW BOOKS
Collins
8 Grafton Street, London
1984

Willow Books
William Collins & Sons plc
London . Glasgow . Sydney
Auckland . Toronto . Johannesburg

First published in Great Britain 1984
© Sharron Davies 1984

Davies, Sharron
Sharron Davies
1. Davies, Sharron   2. Swimming
I. Title   II. Severs, Malcolm
797.2′1   GV837

ISBN 0 00 218120 7

Filmset in Monophoto Ehrhardt by
Ace Filmsetting Ltd, Frome, Somerset
Printed and bound in Great Britain by
Wm Collins & Sons plc, Glasgow

*This book is dedicated
to my family and friends
without whom none of this
would have been possible.*

CONTENTS

CHAPTER ONE

A Packet of Maltesers

Having been a Davies for nearly 22 years now, I am convinced that it is necessary to be just a little mad to be one. There is more than a hint of a soap opera about my family and each of us has added his or her bit to the overall eccentricity. All of us, but my Dad and myself most of all, are like terriers. We hang on and on for dear life but quickly move on to new things when the need or desire has gone. The story of my swimming career is, largely, the story of my family's unorthodox behaviour.

When I was born on 1 November 1962 (after having very inconsiderately kept my poor mother in labour until 3 a.m.), my Dad, Terry, was serving with the Navy. We had a cosy though modest living in that heart of Navyland, Plymouth, and for the first few years my life was 'normal' by any stretch of the imagination. Dad was away at sea much of the time and my mother, Sheila, brought me up quietly in our house close to the centre of the city. It was a suburban life with the highs limited to my father's visits home on leave. Nine months after one of these leaves my twin brothers Mark and Tony were born. I was four at the time and that event was easily the most exciting thing that had happened to me. We were an ordinary, unexceptional, almost humdrum family. However, these doldrums were not to last.

While serving in the Far East, my father developed an eye problem that was serious enough for him to be repatriated back to England. Navy doctors in Plymouth treated him for a callous which had formed on the back of his eye and, after months of care, it was thought that the eye was on the mend and that his sight would correct itself.

However, when washing his hair one day, some of the shampoo

went in his eye. The liquid aggravated the already damaged tissue and he was admitted to Plymouth's Royal Eye Infirmary. The treatment was long and often painful but in the end it was unsuccessful and my father lost both the sight of his eye and his job in the Navy. The doctors stitched his eye together in the hope that in five years' time he might be able to receive more advanced treatment; this never happened.

Naturally, it was a great shock to both him and my mother. For a short period they considered taking the shampoo company to court but soon realized that it would be useless as the liquid had irritated an existing condition; it had not created the problem itself. They also agonized over the thought that, perhaps, the eye could have been saved if he had been sent to see one of the top eye specialists in London.

My father, however, is a pragmatist. Once he realized there was nothing he could do he put 'what-might-have-beens' behind him and concentrated on the immediate problem of how to support a wife, four-year-old daughter and newly-born twins.

Stoic though he was, it was impossible to understand the extent to which this episode was a disaster for him. Not only had he lost a job that he loved he also had to say goodbye to his own long standing sporting ambitions. He had been an excellent shot – he had shot for England at Bisley – and was a competent hockey player but now he was relegated permanently to the sidelines. His bad luck, though, proved my good fortune. Had he not suffered from that eye problem it is unlikely that I would ever have made it as a swimmer. Once I started to show promise he transferred all his frustrated sporting ambitions to me and I really had to do well – for both of us.

Finding another job, however, proved very difficult. He had enjoyed the discipline of the Navy and was a regimented man. Looking for a job in civilian life that offered the responsibilities and challenges of the Navy was not easy. After dozens of interviews and disappointments he realized that if he worked for someone else he would have to slot in at a very subordinate level. He would be on the receiving end of orders instead of dispensing them and that was not at all to his taste.

Added to that there was the problem of his disability. They say

Aged five with Grandad and my pet rabbit Floppy

that in the land of the blind the one-eyed man is king but it seemed that everyone in Plymouth had 20/20 vision and there was no place for a one-eyed former sea dog.

But Dad was not one to give up. He realized that if he was to achieve what he wanted he would have to do it on his own and so he set himself up in business as a breeder of table rabbits. He had no previous experience but the Davies's terrier instinct took over. He read all the books he could find about his new subject and threw himself into it. The prospect of failure just did not occur to him.

What was a period fraught with problems and anxieties for my parents, however, was a time of pure bliss for me. We now had a small farm and animals and I, as quite a tomboy, was in my element. Never in my life have I had any time for dolls or the other usual girlish passions. I liked to be out-of-doors and from the very beginning I was a water baby. Even at the age of two I can remember being taken to the pool yet I cannot recall being afraid of the water for a single moment. On one occasion at the Drake Naval Barracks pool in Plymouth (where I was later to do much of my training) I casually jumped off the diving board into the deep end. It would have been all right if I could swim but no one had bothered to tell me that it was necessary. My poor father, who had witnessed this apparent act of self-destruction, had to jump in to fish me out and save me from drowning. But though he had an awful fright I can't remember feeling any fear. Somehow I felt at home in the water and, even though I could not swim, I felt a strange pull towards it: I loved the feeling of it.

Our house at the time was in the Milehouse area of Plymouth, very close to the Central Park swimming pool. I had a young friend who was being taught to swim there and my mother, who was very keen for me to learn to swim, if only to stop me from killing myself, encouraged me to join my friend in the lessons.

Together we learned with the Devonport Royal Swimming Association. They taught us by tying ropes around our stomachs and dragging us up and down the pool while we tried to catch canes that were being held in front of us.

Although it sounds primitive, it was an efficient method and, before very long, I was able to struggle a few yards with my feet off the bottom. Indeed swimming was rather like everything else – the first full width was the worst. I remember mine well. The torture of making those 15 or so yards is as vivid today as it was then; perhaps because, when it was all over, I received my first ever swimming prize – a packet of Maltesers.

Like all children once the basics had been mastered there was no holding me back and I progressed at the speed of light. Width classes became length classes and after a year I could swim quite well and was taking part in small club events.

My success in the pool, however, was not reflected in my father's business. From determined but inexperienced beginnings he had built up the rabbit business and had prospered to such an extent that he became Britain's biggest exporter of table rabbits but, in 1968, disaster struck in the form of myxomatosis. Almost overnight a profitable business was reduced to ruins and Dad had to change the course of his life yet again. This time he went into the frozen food business and he was one of the first suppliers of frozen portions, particularly chicken. But good idea or not the business never really took off and my father salvaged what he could and tried again; this time as a mushroom farmer. Unfortunately he did not possess the financial backing required to make it work. He was an unusually determined person and he did all he could to learn from books and the experiences of others but he lacked the money and the resources to give the business a real chance. He was the sort of man who, given the right support, could have succeeded in any field. Sadly, this back-up didn't exist and the mushroom business went the same way as the frozen chicken.

Not to be defeated, and never reluctant to start something new, Dad moved into insurance broking: a field in which he excelled. The success he made of this business is responsible, to a very large extent, for my swimming success. For most of my career I was floating just as much on my father's insurance earnings as I was on the water.

Real swimming success, however, did not come overnight. I was not one of those prodigies who go from being a non-swimmer to a gold medal winner within the blink of an eye. I was quite proficient and I loved swimming but I didn't actually win a race – over a width as it happens! – until I was eight. But even then I could feel the hungry need to win stirring within me. I remember once being beaten by a girl called Liz who was my best friend at the swimming club and I determined then and there not to let it happen again. I could not see the point of swimming in races unless they were swum to win. Liz's victory over me had annoyed me and, perhaps for the first time, winning became the most important thing in my life: certainly Liz never beat me again.

Circumstances alter and attitudes gradually change towards most things, but if there was a moment when I changed from being a recreational swimmer to a dedicated competitor this was it. I started to train regularly three times a week with the Devonport Royal Swimming Association and, before very long, took on Devon County training sessions as well. Eventually a coach called Ray Clements began to take me for a few morning sessions, in addition to evening training, but my goal lay elsewhere – I wanted to join an elite squad trained by a marvellous coach named Ray Bickley.

The Devonport club that I belonged to was not the main club in the area. That honour belonged to the Port of Plymouth Swimming Club and Ray Bickley was the club coach. He was a very fine trainer, particularly in technique, and my father had tried to persuade him to allow me to join his squad. It was not easy. Ray was very careful about who he accepted into his select group but, either because he saw some potential in me or because he was worn down by my father's persistent requests, he allowed me to train with him at Port of Plymouth.

All this talk of training must make it appear as if I could go along to a pool and train any time I liked. Not so. Plymouth is not badly off for swimming pools but they are all public pools and the authorities will allow the swimming clubs to take them over only when public demand is low – early in the morning and late at night.

In those earliest days training started with an hour of Devon County Club sessions between 7 and 8 p.m. When it was over I would go to the showers with three other Devonport girls where we would stay for about an hour and a half. It was the warmest place to be and we had to wait until the club session between 9 and 10 p.m. before we could get back into the water again.

For an eight-year-old it was a great adventure. Being allowed to stay up with friends until ten at night in a swimming pool was enormous fun. My father obviously was not keen on me staying up so late but it was the only way we could squeeze in the proper training. The authority's view was that, as it was a public pool, it must be open to the public at the most convenient times. This meant that if we wanted to swim and train outside the special club times we had to fit in with everyone else and pick our way through a pool often choked with recreational swimmers. As I progressed, of course, I wanted to spend more and more time in the water and, though it is true that I was able to find some pool time each day, the conditions were far from ideal. Those of us who did succeed did so despite the conditions, not because of them.

In those early days my training required about two miles of swimming a day but it wasn't just length after boring length – gradually becoming slower. Instead we might do ten 100-metre swims one after the other with just a few seconds of rest in between. The purpose was to build up strength and speed. I had an advantage in that I also went to ballet classes and this had made my legs in- credibly strong. I could beat any of the 17-year-olds in kicking ability and I have to thank ballet for it. Eventually, of course, I had to give up dancing. I enjoyed it immensely and had reached the elementary grades but there came a time when I couldn't study both. Ballet classes were usually just before swimming and it was becoming ridiculous: I just didn't have any time. It was too much for a young schoolgirl to rush home from school, do homework, go to first ballet and then swimming. Apart from the obvious strain on me there was the strain on my parents as they were the ones who had to drive me all over the place and it soon became obvious that I was going to have to make a choice. In the event the choice was easy. When it came to the crunch swimming was an easy winner and from eight onwards swimming was the most important thing in my life.

I used to enjoy going horse riding with my grandfather, but eventually, that too had to be discarded. At first it fitted in quite well because we went on Sundays and didn't interfere too much with my training but as swimming took more and more of a hold so the ponies took more and more of a backseat until there was simply no time for them at all. To be honest I didn't find it that hard to give up. Horse riding is second only to motor racing in expense and we didn't have the funds available that would have given me a chance to excel in the sport. As I wanted to excel more than anything I 'played the percentages' and stuck with the pool.

Once that decision was made I really spared no effort and by the time I was nine I was winning quite a few local meets in my age group. The pastime had become very serious and I was improving faster than I could really comprehend. Each time I dived into the water – or so it seemed – I was trimming seconds off my previous best time. It was a period of great excitement for me. There is nothing like success to keep passion for a sport alive and my natural competitiveness made sure that I squeezed every possible ounce of enjoyment from my sport. It had, of course, become more than just a sport – it was my life. Some girls eat and sleep horses in their formative years; I did the same with swimming. There was never any doubt and I never experienced that 'oh-I-cannot-be-bothered-to-train-today' feeling. It is true that those feelings did creep in later but in those heady first days all moments spent in the water were treats.

Perhaps the luckiest thing for me though was that my father was as keen as I was. He was the one who rose at dawn with me and the sparrows for early training and he was my main source of encouragement. Our daily routine began at six with a huge breakfast of five scrambled eggs and toast before driving to the pool. After an hour and a half of solid training Dad would drive me home for another breakfast – light this time – before I ran, literally, to school. We had Red Setters then and Dad and I would both run with them to the school gates. Because I was in training I was allowed to miss morning assembly and we timed our arrival for 9.20 a.m. – nearly three and a half hours after getting up.

Fortunately, from the beginning I never had to worry about my diet. I was always tall for my age. At 13 I was five foot seven inches and at 15 I was five foot eleven inches; the height I am today. This meant that I could eat virtually anything. It didn't matter how much I ate, my body would either burn it off or grow it off almost immediately. I always had plenty of liver and steak and that type of food –

high protein body-building foods – and my parents always insisted that I came home from school at lunchtime so that they could make sure I ate properly. Later when I was at Plymstock Comprehensive this became rather difficult as it took me 20 minutes to walk home leaving ten minutes to eat only. Even so my parents never relented and I was always required home for lunch. In the evening there would be another cooked meal before training: a total of four cooked meals a day. At 14 I rebelled and refused to eat red meat simply because I hated it. It meant that my parents found it more difficult to devise a balanced diet but they always managed somehow. I must have cost them a small fortune.

Indeed if I owed my future success to anything it was to the dedication of both my parents. I have a great deal to thank my mother for as it was she who organized my home life and was always there when I needed her. Both my parents were always enthusiastic and they made every sacrifice so that I was able to have whatever I needed. Without them and Ray Bickley, Sharron Davies would have been just another also-ran.

Being accepted into Ray's Port of Plymouth squad was one of the many watershed points of my career. Ray was the only proper swimming coach in the whole of the West Country and in his squad were two people I idolized: Debbie Johns and Shaun Penprase. Debbie and Shaun were *the* swimmers in our area. Debbie would win all the girls' events and Shaun would dominate the boys': to me they represented the pinnacle of success in the sport. Both Debbie and Shaun were in Ray's squad and I just had to belong to the same team. They were both members of the National Youth Squad and, though they were not the best swimmers in that squad, just being able to train with junior internationals was great encouragement to me.

Before Ray accepted me into his select little group I used to watch from the side, green with envy for those he was coaching. During early morning training my club, Devonport, had one of the outside lanes of the pool but Ray's Port of Plymouth squad trained in the centre, equivalent to the pole position in motor racing. Nothing mattered to me more than being able to use those centre lanes. Fortunately, my father's ever growing interest in the art of coaching led him to have long conversations with Ray Bickley and it was the friendship that built up between them that finally gained me a place in the squad.

Ray worked with me rather like a potter with raw clay. He corrected all my bad habits and he developed me into a four-stroke swimmer. Like most swimmers in Britain I had started as a breast-stroker before moving into backstroke. Ray laid the foundations of the medley swimmer that was to blossom later.

As I developed, my father realized that I needed experience of different types of competition and he decided to spend his money on gaining me that experience abroad. As Ray was my coach Dad paid for him to go as well and, together, we began to accumulate the racing miles. Sometimes we would go abroad as an individual entry to a European competition but, more often, my father would find a club from another part of the country that had entered and arrange for me to be attached to the club just for the competition.

I remember one occasion when I was about 12 on one such visit to Geneva. Naturally for youngsters of that age, there were chaperones to keep things under control and it was strictly forbidden for the boys to go into the girls' rooms. However, rules were made only to be broken. After dinner one evening, about six girls and six boys were in my room when the chaperone knocked on the door. There was instant panic. One boy hid under the bed, another jumped into the wardrobe and two scrambled for some hiding place in the bath-room. The other two jumped out of the window and hung from the sill – even though the room was three floors up! When the chaperone came in all that was visible was a group of girls on the bed playing cards. She said goodnight to us and, just before leaving, added wryly: 'goodnight boys'.

As something of a tomboy I was interested in mainly adventurous pursuits and it landed me in more than my fair share of trouble. When I was about eight I fell out of a tree-swing in some woods and broke both my arms. As I hit the ground my watch flew off my wrist and I knew that my arms were broken, one quite badly; I could see the ends of the bones contorting my arms into strange, staircase-like shapes. My father was at the farm with the only car so the friend who was with me left me lying on the ground and ran off to telephone for help. I knew Dad would not have a clue where to look for me in the wood so I carefully stood up and with extreme pain picked up my watch and walked out into the open. When Dad found me he was shocked. He tended to be squeamish anyway and he told me to support the obviously broken arm with the other one but he went a pale shade of green when I told him I couldn't as that was broken as well. He was terribly upset at the idea that his precious little daughter had been wandering around in the woods with two badly broken arms. But squeamish or not he was a practical man and he strapped them up with bits of wood as splints and rushed me to hospital where the bones were set under anaesthetic. Unfortunately the bones began to knit in the wrong places and I had to pay another visit to the operating theatre to have my arms rebroken and reset.

In all I spent about six weeks in hospital with my arms in traction but as soon as I was allowed home, despite the fact that my arms were still in plaster, I was back running with the plasters weighing down my arms. I had been a bit worried while in hospital because my arms had always been the weak link in my swimming. The ballet had helped my legs but my arms needed strengthening and I was worried that the accident may have set me back too far.

So once out of hospital we wrapped my plasters in plastic bags and I took to the water for kicking training and then went running, with the plasters weighing down my arms, to build up my arms and shoulders.

As soon as the plasters came off, of course, I threw myself back into full training with a vengeance: with almost immediate success. Within just a couple of months I won my first Devon Championship.

The fall from that tree, however, was not the only scrape I had as a child. I was constantly putting myself in situations that frightened my parents rigid.

On one occasion when I was about five and my father had just started the frozen chicken business, I jumped, presumably for fun, from the upstairs window of our house: about 25 feet from the ground. At the time we had chicken troughs, metal contraptions with metal bars sticking dangerously from them, all around the house. I could easily have landed on one and impaled myself but fate must have been on my side as I landed in soft mud between two troughs and only a foot or so away from a concrete verge. I picked myself up unscathed apart from a few grazes and a mouthful of mud.

Apparently I had been watching Billy Smart's Circus on television and decided to try something death defying myself. It is a miracle that my swimming career was not ended then and there and it is ironic that the only emergencies were the two cases of near heart failure for my parents.

Most parents, I am sure, would have given up on a child so determined on self-destruction; but not mine. Indeed just the opposite. From the moment my serious competitive swimming started, my father devoted all the family money to my career. From that moment on we never had a holiday. There simply was not enough left over in the kitty after my swimming had been paid for. Even my brothers accepted it. No one uttered as much as a moan about not being able to go somewhere exotic. I had total family support. No swimmer could have had a better family.

Even the ordinary things that most families take for granted – new cookers, washing machines and so forth – all went by the board with us. Every last halfpenny was spent on Sharron.

CHAPTER TWO

Aiming for the Olympics

The trips we made abroad for competitions were, quite definitely, the highlight of my training. Once I joined Ray Bickley and Port of Plymouth, club visits abroad became a regular feature of our training and race programme. The first trip I ever made was to a little town just outside Paris and for me it was like winning the pools. We had to travel the cheapest way and that meant by coach. The journey was never ending. We had to drive from Plymouth to Dover, take the ferry to Calais and then drive to Paris. For a ten-year-old it was exhausting but, like most of the kids, I was keyed up with excitement. We stayed with friends of the swimming club we were competing against and I was billeted with a really lovely family who, for years after, came to see me whenever I was competing in France. They couldn't speak a word of English and I couldn't speak a word of French but we still managed to get on famously. When we arrived at their house for that first visit they had somehow found out it was my birthday and they had made me a huge birthday cake. Unfortunately I didn't eat cake and with the insensitivity that only a ten-year-old can muster, I told them so. I didn't really quite understand just how offensive I was being but I refused to eat a single mouthful. I can see now how mean I was, especially as they had gone to such trouble. But it wasn't just that. As well as baking the cake they had turfed their own daughter, Murielle, out of her bedroom so that I could have it. Poor Murielle had to sleep on the couch!

That trip had an unexpected bonus for me however. In the races I won myself some cameras. The French club were giving the cameras away as first prizes and I arrived back in England weighed down with six of them. I didn't have any trouble deciding what to give as presents for Christmas!

That same year, 1972, saw Mark Spitz dominate the Olympics in Munich. At that age I didn't really appreciate just how good Mark was but I sat in front of the television, goggle-eyed, and resolved that I too would one day swim in an Olympic Games. Watching Mark, and my then heroine Shane Gould, planted the seeds of a painful longing within me. To swim in the Olympics became the ultimate for me – the pinnacle of success – and I set my sights firmly on that supreme of competitions. It wasn't that I was dreaming of becoming a superstar or anything like that. I had no thoughts at the time of winning a medal – that came later – all I wanted to do was to be able to share the atmosphere and special magic that the Games obviously had.

I have since met Mark Spitz and I have to admit that he did not live up to my expectations but this must not detract from the fact that the man had an absolutely brilliant, phenomenal, talent. In 1972, however, I just saw him as a good-looking man who won a fistful of medals at the best competition in the world. He was the man of the hour and I didn't look behind the scenes at the monotonous hours of training and the personal sacrifices he must have made. I should have done, of course, as, though I didn't quite see it in that light then, I was making similar sacrifices myself. All I could see was the end product and I wanted just a little of that glitter for myself.

Perhaps because of the cold, impersonal quality of television, I never idolized Mark Spitz or Shane Gould – certainly not in nearly the same way that I had idolized Debbie Johns and Shaun Penprase in those days before I was accepted into Ray Bickley's squad. Debbie and Shaun were real, I knew them and they were there for me to beat if I was good enough. Spitz was just a remote figure and not part of my everyday existence. Anyway the swimmers were the minor characters only; it was the Games themselves that took the leading role in my eyes.

But, at ten, the Olympics were still a long way off. The ambition to swim in them was always at the back of my mind but I knew I had many miles still to swim before I could take part. However, I knew I was on my way. That Olympics year saw me beat Debbie Johns for the first time. Debbie swam breaststroke for England but at

Devon level she was so big and strong that she used to win every-thing else as well. I had always finished second or third to her and beating her was my target: a target I finally hit in the 200 metres backstroke at the 1972 Devon Senior Championships. I was very chuffed – especially as they were my first senior championships.

Until then I had been swimming in Devon Age Group Cham-pionships but I reached the stage where I used to win everything so easily that there was no challenge left. To find competition I had to test myself in the seniors.

So between my eighth birthday in 1970 and my tenth birthday in 1972 I progressed through the Devonport Royal Swimming Association Age Groups, the Port of Plymouth Age Groups, Port of Plymouth Seniors, Plymouth Age Groups, Plymouth Seniors, Devon Age Groups and Devon Seniors.

They were two whirlwind years and I treasured that Devon Senior win over Debbie as much as I have treasured any of my wins since – especially as I had started that year with a pair of broken arms.

Having captured a Devon County Gold medal the next step was for me to compete at national level and, still aged ten, I entered my first National Age Group Championships (ten and under). The 1973 Age Groups were held at Coventry and it was the first time I had swum in a full-sized 50-metre pool. It looked so huge I could hardly believe it. I had trained all my life in 25-yard pools and I remember my joy on first seeing that shimmering Olympic-sized pool as though it were yesterday. The Coventry pool became, and has remained, my favourite pool in the whole country – indeed Coventry, right up until my retirement, was always the place I most liked to go and compete.

I started those 1973 National Age Groups with a fifth in the 100 metres breaststroke – not bad, I thought – and then followed it with a bronze medal in the 100 metres backstroke. I was ecstatic. I must have worn that medal for three days without taking it off. I would take it with me every time I went to the swimming pool and proudly show it to the security man on the door. He must have been heartily sick of seeing it, as must the poor lady who ran the guesthouse we were staying in.

We always stayed in guesthouses and we had regular ones wherever there was a 50-metre pool, mainly at Leeds, Coventry, Blackpool and Crystal Palace. The advantage of guesthouses over hotels, apart from the matter of expense, was that the owners would usually make us soup, or something similarly light, before we went to compete. Just before a race no one feels particularly like eating – there are always plenty of nervous stomachs – and a sympathetic guesthouse lady with a bowl of home-made soup was always welcome.

At that time competitions were held nearly every weekend during the summer but in winter the competition programme was not nearly so demanding. That period was spent concentrating on endurance training; for cramming in the yardage and working on technique. Winter was the hardest, and the dullest, time for me but it came as a much-needed break for my parents as there was not so much driving. Once the summer competitions were in full swing, however, Dad would drive me all over the country. Sometimes my mother and the twins would come as well but it was difficult as the twins were restless during long car journeys and mostly it was just Dad and me. We were a team; I swam and he financed me!

We did receive some financial assistance in the form of a Council sports' grant. It was a one-off grant for £100 to help towards expenses and it was very welcome but it was just a drop in the ocean. To continue competing, I had to rely on my father.

Finance, of course, was a problem for swimming generally, not only for us. The sport was always short of funds and the clubs were always inventing ways to raise more money. At Port of Plymouth we used to organize sponsored swimming events and, for one of these, the Royal Navy ship, HMS *Mohawk* agreed to sponsor me. If a swimmer managed to raise £100 for the club in one of these events it was considered a major success (the equivalent of about £800 today). After my swim, however, the sailors on the *Mohawk* had to fork out over £600. It was front-page news in the local papers. Together with the Plymouth press I was invited on to the ship to be given the cheque; the first time I had been the centre of attention. My memory now is a little hazy but I can remember the press photographers wanted the sailors to lift me up to take a photograph but all I could think about was fear that my skirt would blow up!

Shortly after my success with the boys on the *Mohawk* I was invited on to the *Royal Yacht Britannia* to be introduced to the Queen and the Duke of Edinburgh; and I almost made a hit with them too – literally. The yacht was in Plymouth for a visit and all of us swimmers (and representatives of other sports as well) had to queue up on the deck waiting to be ushered in for the Royal handshake. When my turn came, I tripped over the bottom of the door and almost landed at their feet. I was excruciatingly embarrassed and flushed bright red. The Queen and the Duke of Edinburgh just smiled and made light of it but I wished the deck would open up and swallow me whole.

Although swimming was taking up most of my waking day it would be unfair to give the impression that there was no room for anything else in my childhood life. There were other entertainments and one of my favourites was fishing. Together with my grandfather, I was a member of the Co-op Fishing Club and we used to go out to the Eddystone or a wreck to fish. I liked the sea and I liked the fishing but I could never take the fish off the hooks or put the worms on; Grandad had to do all that. He would put the redgill on the hook and I would sling it over the side and catch the fish. Once I caught one I would have to hold it out at pole length for Grandad to remove from the hook (some fisherwoman!). The fishing was perfect relaxation for me but, in true Davies's style, there was one occasion when it was far from relaxing. As Grandad and I were returning to port in our little boat we were rammed by a large trawler. We sat shouting but watching helplessly as the huge bow of the trawler came bearing down on us. It must have been on automatic pilot. Certainly no one saw us until it was too late. They did make a frantic effort to avoid us at the last minute but succeeded only in giving us a glancing blow instead of cutting us in half. In the event we had to count ourselves lucky with getting away with little damage to the boat – it could so easily have been a full-scale tragedy.

That incident did not dampen our fishing ardour, however. I would go out with Grandad every time I could and I won several fishing trophies, including Fish of the Month! Once I was even

Proudly displaying my catch after a fishing expedition with Grandad

given starbilling in the local press after catching a large bag of huge cod and pollock in one day. Those fish, all over 25 pounds, seemed as big as me and I was very proud when I saw my catch (Grandad's really, as I could hardly lift the fish let alone take them off the hooks) immortalized on the Plymouth front pages.

But even fishing eventually fell victim to the rampant imperialism of swimming. Ray Bickley gradually faded out of the picture and Dad took over as my coach. It was a smooth takeover and, as Dad had been taught as much by Ray as I had, he continued the same programmes. Indeed the two of them had worked together so closely that it was quite natural for Dad to take over on Ray's retirement. I didn't notice much change other than the fact that Dad began to arrange more trips abroad for experience – and run his own finances flat.

Of course as I became increasingly well-known in the sport, I reached the stage where I didn't have to buy my own equipment, but as a youngster starting out, the basic necessities like swimsuits, goggles and tracksuits were a constant drain on resources. It came as a great relief to Dad when companies started to give me whatever I needed as a form of advertising for their products.

But it was not just clothing and equipment that kept the money flowing out before I established myself. Land training was an important part of my fitness programme and land training required weights. Very early on my father had arranged for me to train in a Navy gym under a PT instructor called Mick Large. Mick was a wonderful instructor but, like all Navy personnel, he was eventually posted and I was left without the use of any gym facilities. My father's reaction was immediate. He advertised in all the local papers for weights and he bought all those he could find. They came in all shapes and sizes and in all conditions. Some looked as though they had spent a hundred years or so at the bottom of the sea but Dad didn't mind. He started work with a wire brush and a pot of paint and, before long, we had a full set of perfectly adequate weights in the house. All that was left was to turn the sitting room and the garage into a gym and start work. But it was not so simple. The sofa would have to be moved on to the table and all the furniture moved so that there was enough space to move. On the three evenings of the week when the sitting room to gym transformation took place, weights, totally invisible beforehand, would appear from every nook and cranny. Weights would emerge from under the sofa, from the cupboards, from the sideboard drawers and even some of the furniture, like the leather pouffes, became weight machines in their own right.

Because weight training can be devastatingly boring if it is done alone a friend, Port of Plymouth swimmer Jane Kiff, used to come home with me on weight evenings and we would train together. My father would set up a circuit of about 12 exercises between the sitting room and the garage and we each had to do the circuit three times. The exercises didn't look very sophisticated – one of them was simply having weights balanced on the shoulders before stepping up and down on a wooden tool-box – but they were as effective as they were mind numbing. Without Jane I am sure I would not have been able to cope with the rigours of the weight training. She supplied companionship and the odd moment of light relief in what would otherwise have been a lonely and thoroughly miserable routine. I owe Jane a great deal.

Following the 1973 National Age Groups I continued to make progress at an almost alarming rate. At the same Championships the following year I won a silver medal in the backstroke and made it into a special squad called the '1962 Squad' for international under-12 age group swimmers. To be a member of the squad you had to be one of the top two in the country in your event and its first task was to compete against Holland and West Germany in a triangular meet.

It could not have been a prouder moment for me. I was swimming for England and Wales and for the first time considered myself a proper international. That particular match was held at Cheltenham – on home territory – but there were a few disappointments as well as successes. When we first received notification of where to go, we were all asked to take a black pair of tracksuit bottoms and a white 'T' shirt as a 'uniform'. If we didn't possess these, said the letter, we should take the closest we had to it. Naturally, when the England and Wales team finally assembled it was a motley crew indeed. The asked-for black tracksuit bottoms turned out to be almost every dark colour except black and the 'T' shirts, though they were invariably white, had printing on them in all the colours of the rainbow. It was a shambles. Holland and West Germany were both smartly kitted out with proper tracksuits and we felt very unimpressive and shoddy beside them. The newspapers picked it up and compared us unfavourably with our opponents and the ASA was the subject of some Fleet Street criticism. It all served to deepen our humiliation – especially as the other teams were staying in smart hotels and we were scattered around in guesthouses. The only silver lining was that, of all the England and Wales swimmers, I was the only one to win anything. I won three events and though, as a team, we came a poor last, I felt I had pulled my weight and it went some way to overcoming the general embarrassment. Even so it was not the most encouraging way to start a career as a British international. Everything seemed so second rate; for the first time I learned that the ASA was putting home swimmers at a disadvantage before they even entered the pool. On the rare occasions that Britain has done well in swimming it is despite rather than because of the system. I find it surprising that we have any champions at all.

For that particular triangular meeting we didn't even train as a national squad. The West Germans and the Dutch had been together as squads and were full of pride at the thought of representing their countries. We lacked that strong team spirit and it showed.

There may have been a lack of zest in the national under-12s but there was certainly no lack of competitive spirit in the Davies camp. I had now made the psychological transition from being just a good child swimmer to being one who could capture medals in all-comer races. I was beginning to develop more confidence and was selected to represent England again at the return meet of the Holland, West Germany, England match; this time in Holland. Press criticism from the Cheltenham fiasco had had its effect and this time we were supplied with uniform tracksuits – but only for two days – we had to hand back the tracksuits as soon as we returned to Britain. Still it was an improvement and we were beginning to feel more like a national team. We had more success in the pool this time but again I was the only one to bring back a medal but at least there was the feeling that the ASA was trying to do something to boost our morale.

All this was in 1975 when I was still only 12 years old. It sounds awfully young to be representing England and gadding about all over Europe but, for reasons which I still don't fully comprehend, swimmers seem to grow up quicker than most other children. Perhaps it is the discipline of training, I don't know, but we all seemed to be very precocious and mature kids and we already had a sense of direction in our lives. Certainly at 12 I was thinking much more for myself than most of my schoolfriends seemed to be.

Early the following year I was selected for the Green Shield National Youth Squad. It was a squad for Under 16s so many were considerably older than me but my swimming was really beginning to come together. With this squad I went to Luxembourg where I managed to break the British Junior record for the 200 metres backstroke. It was my first record that meant anything at all and it was the incentive I needed in my quest for national senior honours. I captured that record in February and it carried me through on a high to the National Short Course Championships in April. Short Course is just swimming jargon for a small pool but it was a National Championship and I was competing against seniors: the best swimmers in the country. There were no miracles – I didn't suddenly become a rags to riches swimmer – but I did bag a bronze medal in the 200 metres backstroke and I knew that better performances were not too far away. I was quite content with my first real taste of senior competition.

My main memory of that competition, however, is not very adult at all. The routine at the Championships was to swim heats in the morning, rest in the afternoon and swim the finals at night. Most people try to sleep in the afternoon but I have never been able to do that – if I sleep in the middle of the day it means I must be ill – and my habit was to read comic magazines. As it was a Championship I was unable to eat much because of nerves but I loved fruit and my father used to fill melons with glucose and I would eat them while I was reading my comics. Often these comics had competitions that I used to enter and, on this occasion, the competition was about the Diana Ross film *Mahogany*: one of the few films I knew anything about. The upshot was that I won a Diana Ross album – the first and only thing I have ever won outside a swimming pool – for my efforts. My father was delighted with this and the week's success and 'rewarded' me further by buying me the most monstrous pair of gypsy hoop earrings which I chose.

On the swimming front, I was making incredible progress. Almost overnight I had gone from being a Devon 'country-girl' swimmer to being a fairly good young national athlete and now a national senior athlete. I was attaining my goals fast but my main goal seemed just as remote as ever. I didn't envisage myself at the Olympics just yet.

After the Short Course Championships I was invited to a Coca-Cola international in Leeds. It was the first time I had ever been to Leeds, which for a backstroker was a positive disadvantage. The pool there was a full-size, 50-metre Olympic pool but for some strange reason the architect had designed a big diamond shape on the ceiling. This had the effect of causing backstrokers to lose their bearings – I certainly found it virtually impossible to swim in a straight line. It was a full international meeting with most of the European countries present but entry was by invitation only. For some unfathomable reason it didn't qualify as an official international (so I still could not take my Great Britain tracksuit home!) but I knew it was a marvellous chance to do well and impress the selectors. However, all I was able to do in my race was to swim it at a zigzag. Because of the diamond on the ceiling I couldn't keep in a straight line and I kept bouncing off the lane markers. It was embarrassing but I still managed to break the Olympic qualifying time and for the first time I could really see light at the end of the Olympic tunnel.

However there were three of us who were all about the same in ability and age – Joy Beasley, Kim Wilkinson and myself – and we all competed in the same event. We were all progressing at roughly the same rate and we all seemed to take our turn at winning. We were all fighting for an Olympic place – except when we were occasionally beaten by an older girl called Mandy James whose wins caused us to split up. We knew we wouldn't all go to the Olympics and that the final selection would hinge on the results of the National Championships that followed close on the heels of the Coca-Cola. In the interval, however, I went to as many invitational meets as I could. Being an Olympic year it wasn't just a case of winning races, it was also a case of realizing the Olympic qualifying times. Although I had broken the time for the 200 backstroke at Leeds I knew I needed to continue doing it if possible so that the selectors would not be in any doubt.

In many ways I had to try harder than the others simply because I was born in November. At the age of 12 or 13 the body is growing and building itself up very quickly. This meant that those who were born in January or February were significantly bigger and stronger than me. At 15 or 16 everything has levelled out and it doesn't matter anymore but in those years of puberty I had to put in that much more effort just to maintain whatever edge I had over the opposition.

Even though I had met the Olympic qualifying times I was not certain, by any means, of an Olympic place. The other girls had also met the time and I knew that final selection would rest on the results of the National Championships. It was a curious time for me. I travelled to the Championships with my father and Jane (my home gym companion), remarkably unbothered by it all. Although I knew that, provided I swam well, I had a reasonable chance of being chosen, another part of my mind refused to accept it as even a possibility. It was as though I had already made up my mind that the other girls would go to Montreal and I would go to the next Olympics.

My only real chance of selection was in the 200 metres backstroke. There were four of us in the race who had bettered the qualifying time and I had to be in the first three to have a chance: I made it by three hundredths of a second.

But it wasn't until I arrived back in Plymouth after the competition that I was told I had been selected. It was in the newspaper: front page. Apparently I was the youngest ever to be selected for Britain and the press started to hound me for a story. Almost everywhere I went there were photographers and reporters. It made me feel terribly important and, at 13, I was flattered by all the attention. My father didn't allow my ego to become too inflated, however. His view was that we had only just made it and that there was much work left still to do. He did his best to protect me from the worst excesses of the press – he became very angry and almost forcibly evicted them from the pool on a couple of occasions – and the hard training he insisted on left me no time to raise my feet more than an inch off the ground anyway.

I was, naturally, absolutely thrilled. When I am asked now what was it like going to those Olympics, my stock reply is 'fantastic'. This is not because I lack the vocabulary or just cannot be bothered to answer the question in detail – it is simply because I don't remember very much about the Games. From the moment I heard I had been selected until the time the team returned to England my head was in the clouds. It was all a bit of a dream – a dream that did not end until I was accumulating the mileage in Plymouth again looking towards the Edmonton Commonwealth Games.

Even the training, which Dad always insisted came before all else, didn't burst my bubble. In some ways, of course, I was lucky being hidden away in Plymouth – away from the centre of the national press in London. *Nationwide* came down from London to film and talk to us but my father allowed them only three minutes and sent them packing at the end of it. They were annoyed and wanted more time but Dad could never be dissuaded and he refused ever to allow my training routines to be upset by unwanted attentions. If we had been living in London it would have been that much more difficult to keep them at bay and the whole episode may well have gone to my head. As it was, I was just delighted to be going and determined to give my very best for my country. Perhaps for the first time in my life, I felt very patriotic.

CHAPTER THREE

Montreal

Three weeks before the departure date for Montreal, all the Olympic swimmers met up at Crystal Palace for an intensive training camp and to be fitted out with all the uniforms and gifts that are the perks of national selection. Unlike the old days when any old tracksuit and 'T' shirt would do, this time I found myself being properly measured by a tailor for a uniform that would be for my use only. But despite my continued feeling of elation I do remember clearly my disappointment at the style of the uniform (obviously such considerations are very important to a young teenage girl). It was awful – rather old fashioned – and I felt a little embarrassed at wearing it. Naturally my pride at being in the team did much to overcome any qualms I felt on the fashion front; as did the pampering we received from the commercial sponsors of the team. Towelling manufacturers would supply us with towels, the girls received parcels of make-up and there were training shoes, bags, toiletries – you name it we had it. In all it took about two suitcases just to hold the handouts. I was too young to understand fully why people were giving us all these things but obviously it was very nice and made me feel of some consequence. If nothing else, we were well enough equipped to go off and do our bit for Britain.

However, these luxuries were more than counterbalanced by the spartan conditions at Crystal Palace. Crystal Palace, as a national sports centre, has a hostel for visiting athletes and it was this hostel which became our home for three weeks. It was a cross between a boarding school on the verge of bankruptcy and an Army barracks for basic training. There was a large central cafeteria – very impersonal and with food to match – and the bedrooms, more like small dormitories really, were nothing if not austere. It was an eye-opener for me but it did nothing to diminish my excitement.

Posing for the newspapers with another 13-year-old swimmer, Joy
Beasley, at the Olympic training camp in Crystal Palace, June 1976
Associated Newspapers

Because Joy Beasley (who was also 13 but a few months older) and I were so young we were constantly being invited to give interviews and be photographed for radio and television; the ubiquitous gents from Fleet Street were hanging around us like bees round a honey pot. Joy looked as grown up as I felt; years and years of gruelling training had not allowed her much time for a normal childhood either. Yet the press photographers were anxious to surround us with dolls and teddy bears to emphasize our youth before photographing us. Joy and I, of course, didn't have any teddy bears – but the photographers would always bring a bag of stuffed fluffies with them and we would be required to cuddle these things while they clicked away. Needless to say Joy and I found this attitude very annoying.

One of the more enjoyable media interviews that Joy and I experienced during those final three weeks was a guest appearance on the *Blue Peter* children's programme. We were interviewed by Lesley Judd and given gold *Blue Peter* badges and we left that studio feeling quite 'grown up' instead of the babies of the team. I've had a soft spot for *Blue Peter* ever since.

Much of it, of course, was above my head and my memory of it now is far from clear but I do remember that, whenever a camera or a microphone was held in front of me, I was never at a loss for words. The thought of being heard or seen by millions of people never made me nervous and the interviewers never had to struggle to keep me saying something! Words just tumbled out and it was probably then that I first began to think of journalism – particularly TV journalism – as a possible career.

Leaving for Montreal turned out to be quite a performance. We all had to wear our official blue trouser suits and line up for countless photographic sessions. It seemed forever before we finally saw the inside of the aeroplane but, when we did, the first thing to do was to form a queue at the lavatory door so that we could change out of those restricting uniforms and into some comfortable old jeans for the flight. The journey time was about eight hours so it was important that we were comfortable for at least some of the time. Of course before landing in Montreal we all started queueing up again as we had to be clad in our official 'finery' for our arrival.

I found it all fascinating. The adventure of my first trans-Atlantic flight was also terribly exciting. The meals, the film and the atmosphere were all new; it really made me feel that I was embarking on something special and the eight hours of that flight were over in a flash for me.

The swimming events are always very early in the Olympic programme so there were only swimmers on our particular flight. This meant that we were the first people to arrive and the first to settle into the fabulous Olympic Village that had been built. Many competitors complained that the living quarters were cramped but I didn't find them so at all. We were all allocated flats which were to be sold as apartments when the Games were over. The swimming girls had two of these flats with three girls in one room, four in another and six in the largest one. On paper this must seem that those who complained were justified but, in fact, there was more than enough room for everybody. The flats were well designed and the bunk beds were arranged so that there was plenty of space to move around and store belongings. There was a good bathroom and sitting area (with a television) and I found it all more than satisfactory. Of course as a 13-year-old I wasn't as concerned with privacy as some of the older ones might have been so the communal style of living didn't bother me – indeed, if anything, I found it fun.

In fact, I found the whole experience exhilarating. The village arrangements were two large men's blocks and one women's block. As usual the women were allowed in the men's block but not vice versa. There was a rule that was tolerant of women who were discovered in men's bedrooms but it was not permissible for men to 'compromise' the women in any way. It was of course, grossly sexist but that is the way the minds of sports administrators work. So, in order that the men didn't stray anywhere near the forbidden fruit the team headquarters was situated in the men's block – quite some trek away from where we were living. Needless to say the question of who was allowed in whose block did not hold the slightest interest for me. I was too young and interested only in the swimming. Others in the team, however, were mainly concerned with having a good time. They were team 'passengers' in many ways and if there was any trouble they were the ones who were usually in the thick of it.

To name any of them would be unfair but they annoyed me. In my view they didn't take the games seriously enough and they didn't seem to be as dedicated as people representing their country perhaps should. I did not feel particularly strongly about it in Montreal – I was after all too young – but as my career developed I came to have less and less time for the sporting parasites and I was never slow in coming forward to tell them what I thought of them.

In Montreal, however, there was too much new to see to have time for criticism. Just something as simple as the dining hall was a place at which to marvel. It was huge and catered for every taste. Every type of fruit, every national dish and any food you could possibly wish could be cooked any way you wanted. I used to sit, fascinated, in that dining hall for hours just watching the people milling around. The whole world seemed to have come together in it. There were nationalities that I had read about only in books before and it made me realize, perhaps for the first time, that I really was attending a world games.

I was young and impressionable but that dining hall will always stay in my mind. It seemed to represent the essence of the Olympics. It is a feeling I shall treasure because the next Olympics I was to attend didn't create the same harmonious atmosphere at all.

To me that Montreal village was more like a city than a village. It was open 24 hours a day and there was always something happening. One of the reasons why I didn't appreciate the complaints of lack of space in the apartments was because it was unnecessary to spend much time in them. The general rooms on the lower floors – day, video and fitness rooms – meant that the only time you actually needed to be in your apartment was when the time came to sleep. Even the dining hall was open 24 hours a day.

There was a swimming pool in one of the men's blocks and, quite soon after our arrival in the village, I was in the lift, fully clothed after visiting the headquarters, when Duncan Goodhew and Philip Hubble decided I should take a dip in this pool then and there. Before I really realized what was happening they had thrown me into the pool, clothes and all.

Under normal circumstances it wouldn't have mattered. Clothes dry soon enough and it's all just a good laugh.

Unfortunately this was the Olympics and the Olympic organizers are very security conscious. At the Munich Olympics four years earlier they had had the horror of the attack on the Israeli team and the Canadian authorities were determined that there would be no repetition in Montreal. So in order to keep tags on us and to keep undesirables out we were all required to carry identity passes wherever we went. Mine, of course, had gone into the water with me and, when it finally dried out, the ink had run under the plastic cover and it was almost impossible to read my name. Although it sounds minor, it led to a great deal of trouble being allowed in and out of the village. For some reason it never occurred to them to issue me with a new pass so whenever I wanted to go through a barrier I was held up longer than anyone else while the security officer tried to decipher my pass.

As time went on it did not become easier, even though the guards began to recognize me. Security everywhere was terribly strict; to gain admittance into the living accommodation we had to go through two check points where there were X-ray baggage and body searches. Around the boundary, armed guards were posted every ten yards or so: there were also armed guards on every floor.

For us this was a curse as the female guards communicated with each other by radio and their electronic conversation would continue non-stop. The weather at that time of the year was rather humid and to be at all comfortable at night we had to keep the windows open (covered with fly screens to keep the insects out – something I found hard to become used to) and the curtains open. This was efficient in keeping the bedroom at a reasonable temperature but it also meant we were all woken up at some unearthly hour in the morning when the security guards changed their shifts. Their radios would be blaring out and it was totally impossible to get any sleep at all from then on. No wonder we were always the first down to breakfast and the first into the pool for practice.

The opening ceremony of the Montreal Olympics was one of the most moving experiences of my, albeit short, life. Preparing for it, however, was no easy matter. The British Olympic authorities, in their wisdom, had chosen white Panama hats with wire-stiffened brims for the women to wear. We had had to pack these hats in our luggage for the journey to Canada and when they were pulled out in readiness for the ceremony each hat looked like a totally different Paris creation. They were bent into the most outlandish shapes and many of the girls spent half the night feverishly trying to twist their hats into some sort of reasonable shape. It wasn't very successful and many of the hats were still rather contorted when we marched into the arena; many of us were quite self-conscious about it. I have to admit that, from a distance and in all the photographs, we looked very smart, but at the time we felt we were the poor relations. A great deal more thought needs to be given to uniform design for national athletes – what looks passable on the drawing board is not often practical and Britain, all too frequently, seems to be the country caught out.

Peculiar hat or not, though, that first day ceremony was genuinely magical. I was standing behind Princess Anne (which made me even prouder) and the people, noise and colour combined with the sheer size of the stadium completely overwhelmed me. Even now when I look at photographs of that opening ceremony with all its athletes and the crowds of cheering people, I feel a rush of pride when I think that somewhere I am among the multitude. It would be impossible to pick me out but of course, I know I was there and it is a marvellous feeling. One of the reasons for this is that the Montreal opening was the one and only one I was to experience. When I competed in the Edmonton Commonwealth Games two years later I was unable to take part in the ceremony because I was swimming the next day and there was no ceremony as such, due to the Afghanistan controversy, at the Moscow Olympics in 1980. Naturally I wasn't to know at the time that it would be my only opening and I am incredibly grateful that it was such a fabulous one. It was one of the most special moments of my life and I shall never forget it. Everything I have ever done in swimming, all the hours of training, all the lost boyfriends, was worthwhile just for that one unforgettable moment. It was blissful.

Being able to carry that memory home was even more important to me than it was for the others because I missed out on the parties and social gatherings that are a feature of the Olympics once the strain of competition is over. I was not actually excluded from any

of the parties but because of my age I also was not given the opportunity to join in. I always had to be the first one in bed and the
chaperones were particularly vigilant in making sure that the three
youngest girls met their curfew time which was an hour before
everyone else. For some reason, however, all swimmers are treated
a little like children irrespective of their age. Our curfew time was
always long before anyone else's and swimmers were constantly
getting into trouble for breaking the rules. It was not really surprising. Any reasonable person would expect, for argument's sake,
a 20-year-old red-blooded male swimmer who had just given his
best for his country in the pool, and who had trained single-mindedly
to be picked in the first place, would want to celebrate just a bit when
it was all over. In any other sport he would have been able to but
swimmers had to revolt if they were to go out and enjoy themselves.
Over the years there have been many such 'rebellions' and one
would have expected that the authorities would have questioned
why and tried to do something about it. It hasn't happened.
Swimming officials still seem to regard all their charges as infants
and seem unable to overcome their blind-spots.

My own father was the same. He found it hard to adjust from
treating me as a child to regarding me as a young woman. In many
ways, of course, I was just a swimmer to him with goals that had to
be achieved. He was working towards a particular championship or
race on which he would concentrate totally. He was unable to
recognize the changes that were taking place in me and he was taken
aback when he found that the little girl he had started out with had
become a young woman. I am sure it is because swimming officials
are also swimming parents that there is this reluctance to accept that
their charges have grown up. It is certainly a problem to which they
need to give a great deal of thought if they hope to solve team
behaviour problems in the future.

Returning to Montreal, I have to mention that the swimming
facilities laid on for us by the Canadians were unbeatable. We swam
in some of the best 50-metre pools I have seen anywhere. They were
all far superior to any pool in Britain (with the possible exception of
Edinburgh – and that is hardly ever used!) and we revelled in them.
One of the pools we used was an open air one by the river and it was

quite luxurious to be able to acquire a suntan while going through the training routines. Some of the pools even had piped music underwater; I considered that a particularly good innovation. It made a two-hour training session that much more bearable and it definitely helped me to forget the aches in my muscles as I worked: you can't ask for more than that.

The Olympic pool was in reality two pools: one for competitions and another one for training. It meant that, once all the changing rooms, shower rooms, press rooms, restaurants, galleries and all the other requisites of an Olympic pool had been added, the complex was literally gigantic. It was so large, in fact, that the Canadians, in a sensible attempt to help people find their way around, had painted different-coloured arrows on all floors. Each colour led to a different place and if it had not been for those arrows I would have lost myself on more than one occasion. We had to carry a colour code book around with us whenever we were in the swimming complex but it was far preferable to getting lost and the system worked brilliantly.

When it was time for my particular heat in the Games I found myself up against a couple of the top East Germans. Swimming heats are organized so that the top seeds – that is the people with the fastest recorded times before the Games – have the advantage of the middle lanes. This is so that they have a chance to see as much as possible of what is happening around them. Being unseeded I was relegated to the outside lane and the competitors who should have been in the two lanes inside me had withdrawn. From my position I could not see anything going on around me in the pool: it was like having a swimming pool to myself.

Even though I knew I faced this disadvantage I could not help being overawed by the occasion. Even for the heats we were marched out into the pool area. Music was blaring, people were shouting and the whole pool area looked as though it was sponsored by Technicolor. No feeling of pride can be quite as exalted as that of marching in for Britain before a race and, despite the fact that I had no high hopes, I was on top of the world.

From the moment we were ushered into the glass-fronted competitors' room two races before my heat I was keyed up and nervous.

From this room we watched the preceding race and then lined-up and marched out to music to take up our positions at the end of the lanes. The secret before a race is to keep the body moving as much as possible; to keep warm and to keep on as many clothes as possible until the whistle goes. Only then should you strip off and get ready for the race. As it was the 200 backstroke we had to dive into the pool straight away but backstrokers always have a habit of hanging back. The reasoning behind this is that if you can be last in the pool you will have the advantage because everyone else has had to wait.

It is ludicrous really as there is no real advantage but psychology is a major part of swimming (as in so many sports) and if you believe it is going to help you will do everything you can to obtain that advantage. Sometimes officials become annoyed at this rigmarole and help us in but it is always a performance.

Once in it was just a quick count of the lane flags to the wall (to assist in timing turns) and one, two, three go. I have to admit that the nervous butterflies were going berserk inside my stomach. I had nothing really to lose and that helped (and I wasn't anywhere near as nervous as I was to be four years later in Moscow) but the adrenalin flow was still strong enough to make me feel a little sick.

I tried to remain as calm as possible by telling myself that I was there to gain experience only. My job was to watch, listen and learn to equip me for future competitions. I was not expected to excel in this one. Indeed I knew I did not stand a chance. Even so I was still determined to do my very best and not let Britain down.

Although I wasn't expecting to qualify for the final I was reckoning on setting a British record. I was improving unbelievably quickly and every time I got into the pool I was knocking seconds off my time and I intended this to be no exception. But I was disappointed. I could manage a time within 0·3 of my previous best only.

All three of the backstroke girls recorded poor times and the reason was that we were children in an adults' team. The training requirements of children are very different from those of adults. Adults can withstand a long tapering-off period before a major competition because their bodies are able to store speed. Younger bodies do not have this ability yet we had had to go along with the same tapering-off period as the older swimmers. I realize it doesn't seem too much of a handicap and it must seem a rather lame excuse but I am convinced that if I had had a shorter taper and the type of training my father would have given me, I could have improved my Montreal time by at least a second and possibly even more.

Despite the poor and disappointing times, however, I still finished the fastest Briton and was nineteenth out of 32 overall. Not a spectacular result but not bad for one who was just competing for the experience. The team was satisfied and I was quite happy but an indication of what could have happened came a few weeks after the Olympics. Once back in England my father trained me again for the Europa Cup and I broke the British record with a time four seconds faster than Montreal!

My father was present at the games in Montreal but he was not allowed to come near me in a coaching capacity. Once in a British squad every swimmer comes under the aegis of official ASA coaches and that is that. My father told the team coaches he disagreed with their methods and tried to impress on them the need to give me more practice but they had their own techniques and refused to listen to him. At 13 I was too young to take the initiative myself and fly in the faces of the official coaches. I took what they said at face value just as I would accept anything my father told me. I knew they were adopting different methods from those of my father but they were national coaches and to be obeyed. It was as simple as that.

There were no serious clashes between my father and the team coaches as Dad was not expecting too much from the trip anyway. He knew I had nothing to lose and that I was learning just by being there. He tolerated the national coaches but he was very critical of them.

It is worth mentioning here that some of the best coaches in Britain do not rise into the exalted ranks of the national coaches. If a good coach upset the highest levels of the ASA for any reason he was simply never asked to take a national squad. In my opinion, Keith Bewley and my father are two of the best British coaches. Keith had trained such swimmers as June Croft, the Osgabys, Gaynor Stanley and several other top swimmers but he was relieved of his duties when he took a national team to Moscow. Keith has frequently had disagreements with the ASA and has been particularly outspoken against the little they spent on the swimmers.

My father understood the system and knew that inferior coaches held the reins but he remained silent because there was not a medal in the offing for me to lose. If I had been a medal prospect and the official coaches had lessened my chances he would have been furious: in fact he would have done his utmost to take me away from them.

Once that race was over, my job in Montreal had been completed but we still had a week to enjoy before the closing celebrations and the flight home. The Canadians were marvellous hosts; they arranged trips for us everywhere. We were taken into the mountains and the lakes and really allowed to enjoy ourselves. At one lake they gave us little two-person sailing craft – a sort of windsurfer – and most of us kept falling off but it was great fun and we kept trying. I was with my friend Kim, one of the other young swimmers, but we were having no luck at all. Every time we got the board upright we seemed to be in the water again. Just as we were mounting the thing for the umpteenth time Duncan Goodhew came bowling along with a superior: 'it's easy, let me show you how to do it.'

Kim and I were only too happy to let him try so we swam over to another boat and let him climb up. Just as he did a bar swung across, hit him on the head and sent him flying into the water. We nearly drowned because we were laughing so much and it was vastly entertaining to see 'old clever clogs' receiving his just desserts for throwing me into the pool and ruining my security pass. Seeing Duncan take his come-uppance made my day.

On another occasion we were let loose with some Red Indian-style Canadian canoes and, being English and quite young and reckless to boot, we tried to cram six into a three-man canoe. Needless to say it became very unstable so I volunteered – because the weather was warm and the water inviting – to get out and swim away. The rest of the team were standing by an old pier on the bank and, as I tried to clamber up the pier to get out, I caught my foot on a rusty piece of metal jutting out below the water line. The gash was deep and almost the whole length of my foot. Blood was everywhere and my team-mates pulled me to the bank and rushed off to call an emergency ambulance. In the meantime another team member who had been playing with some scrambling motor cycles laid on by the Canadians was rushed over to share my ambulance. He had been riding without a shirt and had parted company with the cycle on some gravel. All the skin had been ripped from his back and the ambulance staff had a handful with the two of us. He was yelling and screaming as they dabbed him down with antiseptic and I was yelling and screaming as they tried to put local anaesthetic injections between my toes. It was all quite a performance and when the closing ceremony came around I looked more like a war veteran than a competitor.

The closing ceremony itself was nearly as spectacular as the opening ceremony. I have never, before or since, experienced such an eruption of friendliness and unbridled joy. All the tension of competition was over and the athletes turned that stadium into the venue for a party; it was the most indescribable feeling. No one in that stadium had a care in the world – the atmosphere and genuine sense of comradeship carried us all aloft: in my case I didn't descend until we arrived back in London.

To be able to share that joy with my parents made the day even more exciting for me: and I had the people of Plymouth to thank for it.

The Mayor of Plymouth at the time, Mr Floyd, had set up a fund to enable my parents to come to the Games to watch me. They arranged a polo match between Plymouth Argyle and Port of Plymouth and gave all the money raised to my parents. It was one of those acts of kindness that has left, even now, West Country blood very strong in my veins. I shall be eternally grateful for that gesture: it was the final ingredient for a memorable and enjoyable Olympics.

CHAPTER FOUR

Second Thoughts

Once the Montreal Games were over and I was back in England it was straight back into my father's clutches and flat out training. He sharpened all the swimming edges that had been dulled by the ASA coaches and prepared me for the Europa Cup which was held at Crystal Palace a month or so after our return. The Europa Cup is an important meet – a sort of European Championship for women and my target was the British 200 metres backstroke record. As I have already said I took it easily. The record was broken by four and a half seconds and I swam about five seconds faster than I had in Montreal.

To break a record by that sort of time is to smash it but it has to be remembered that British records in those days were not particularly special. The overall standard had not been very high for a long time and all the records were up for grabs. I am supported in this by the fact that, though I smashed the British record, I could manage no more than a bronze medal in the race. It was almost a silver – the girl who beat me did so by a mere one hundredth of a second – but the East German girl who won it was a clear winner and, though taking the British record was satisfying, I didn't feel the result was an outstanding achievement.

It was encouraging for me, of course, that British records were so attainable at this mid-point of my development. As they were so far below the European and World records I had a sort of half-way house at which to aim. This meant that I always had a goal that I felt was within reach and the despairing feeling that I was never going to make it didn't really have a chance to grow.

It was a pity, though, that the British records were so low for it affected the status of British swimming in the world. The reason for the poorness was largely that British swimmers rarely had sufficient ambition. Most would climb up through the grades and aim, not for an Olympic medal but for just a place in the team. They were what I call trippers; they trained hard enough to be selected, went to the Games and had a good time and then dropped out of the sport. They wanted the fun and prestige of participation in the Games but they were not prepared to continue striving to attain even greater heights. There was no fire in their stomachs – perhaps as much the fault of their coaches as themselves – and they never developed a killer instinct to win.

In my case my father was just as ambitious for me as I was for myself. He would never allow me to relax. Once one hurdle was safely overcome he had me looking squarely at the next one. If I did well there would be smiles and a pat on the back but it never lasted long. I wasn't allowed to bask in my wins and I wasn't allowed to become swollen headed. Dad was constantly reminding me how much slower I was than the top girls in the sport and I was encouraged to aim at them and forget about resting on my laurels. It was a healthy attitude and kept me eager for success: I could never really understand those who gave up with their job half completed.

David Wilkie had done much to dispel the lackadaisical attitude in the men and I was helping to dispel it among the women. After the 1976 team broke up and the 'trippers' retired, Duncan Goodhew, Philip Hubble and I were the nucleus of a far more competitive team. British swimming began to feel some pride in itself again and I was delighted to be a part of it. Helping to raise the standard of British swimming was every bit as thrilling as winning the odd race. Of course big races were something special and, being honest, I have to say I raced them largely for my own satisfaction, but seeing the other girls inspired by me and having to work hard to prevent them catching me was very stimulating. It was like working with a new team and it bolstered my growing feeling that we were going places.

One of the great advantages of this new spirit in the camp was that I started to put together strokes. As I have already mentioned, I started my career as a breaststroker and moved into backstroke and I did not pay much attention to the other two strokes – butterfly and front crawl. With the Olympics over, however, I began to give more thought to these more neglected disciplines and entered a few medley races. To my astonishment I swam very well. It made me realize that my best prospect for the future may not be in backstroke after all, but in a combination of all the strokes – the individual medley: a sort of swimming decathlon.

At about this time, too, I became convinced within myself that an Olympic medal was a definite possibility for me. I was swimming well and improving all the time and I knew I was still a long way from my peak. This was the beginning of 1977 and I was only 14. Already I was capturing senior records (albeit not very elusive ones), but my body had some way to develop; let alone my swimming techniques. Together, my father and I started to look seriously ahead at the Olympics of 1980, only this time I would not be aiming at experience: I would be there to win.

Once I had made this mental commitment I began studying the girls I was going to have to beat – and it was quite depressing. In the main they were East Germans and they were not only much faster than me but they were also on steroid body-building programmes.

The Herculean task of beating a swimmer and a drug was brought into very sharp focus for me at the 1977 European Championships at Jönköping in Sweden. In my event I was third behind two East Germans and it was the same pattern in every other women's event: East Germans first and second and the remainder battling for the bronze. There had to be an explanation other than natural talent and good coaching and that was anabolic steroids; the amazing fact was that its use was so blatant.

For instance, at the European Championships in Rome in 1983, the East German girls took first and second in every single event and yet they didn't have one male winner. Okay, so the evidence is circumstantial but it is damning. No one in the swimming world is in the slightest doubt as to what is going on. If it was simply that they had superior coaches and techniques it would apply to men and women alike, but it does not. They dominate the world in the women's events only, as they do in virtually every sport; it does not affect swimming only.

Quite obviously they are using a steroid – a muscle-building steroid. The effect of these drugs in basic terms is that they enable a woman to develop male characteristics. They convert more energy and protein into muscle than would normally be possible for a woman; in other words they are defying nature.

For instance, if I trained 24 hours a day and competed against a man who trained only six hours a day the man would still build more muscle than me simply because his body is naturally geared towards heavy muscle building. In female bodies the energy and protein is used for different metabolic processes.

So what the East Germans were doing, in effect, was and is for that matter, giving their girls the bodies of athletic males. During the whole of the winter training season the East German girls would be given something to take every morning. I do not believe that the girls ask to take these drugs and I do not believe they are keen to take them but it appears to be the policy of their sports authorities and the girls themselves don't have any choice.

Once they have drunk their morning cocktail of steroids and vitamins they go into the pool and train very hard. No one denies that the East German girls still put in the training hours and that they work terribly hard; it is just that they end up with a man's body for their efforts. The irony is that, when summer competition time comes around again, the East Germans always pass their dope tests. This is because the drugs are used in the winter only when the swimmers are developing their muscle. Once this is over you don't want to build muscle anymore, you want to gain speed, so you stop taking the steroid (after 48 hours only it is no longer detectable in the blood or urine) and concentrate on using the muscle already formed to develop speed. The dope testers are not fooled but what can they do? The East German girls are female genetically, so they cannot be categorized as men, yet they have five o'clock shadows, no breast development, very deep voices and they have very strong thoraxes that have the shape of a man: in other words they do not have a woman's hour-glass shape, they have 'V' shapes.

There could, of course, be random dope testing to sort out this problem but East Germany, the USSR, Hungary, Cuba – in fact all Communist countries – will not allow random, year-round, testing to be introduced; and the international authorities are never allowed inside a Communist country to test outside of properly constituted meetings. In Britain and all other western countries random testing is not only allowed but it is positively encouraged so western swimmers never have the opportunity to become hooked into the steroid bandwagon.

Although I knew about steroids and the effect they had on times and medals I was never tempted. In this country there is a life after swimming and I always had an eye to that future – drugs didn't really fit into it. Apart from being illegal there are many side-effects and one of them is sterility and I very much want to have children so, though I may have given the idea a second thought, it would never have been more than that: in the final analysis the risks were too great.

The drugs were offered to me on many occasions. They are relatively easy to obtain – many body-building gyms have them for sale under the counter (and even the more potent ones that are available on prescription only are still pretty easy to obtain) – and if an athlete was determined to take them and did find them difficult to procure in England all he would have to do would be to buy a quick day ticket across the Channel where they are far more readily available.

But even though they were offered to me, the risks outweighed the so-called advantages and I did not once touch them throughout my career. I suppose I was fortunate in that I am naturally a person of big build – and so perhaps would have benefited from steroids less than some – and my father, anxious though he was for success, would never, even for a moment, have entertained the thought of using them.

The only time I ever used a drug while competing was during my battles with the ASA over professional status. The drug was a simple pain-killer and it is a story I shall discuss in more detail later.

Despite the frustration of having to compete against steroids as well as swimmers at the Jönköping European Championships, which were in the latter half of the year, 1977 was an important year for me.

At the beginning of the year I once again joined the Green Shield

Youth Squad which held a training camp at Crystal Palace over the New Year period. This was some of the most intensive training I had ever done. I increased my swimming output to about four and a half hours a day and I started to give maximum effort. As expected my times started to improve and my confidence increased but I also began suffering more and more from a complaint that had plagued my early days of swimming – nose bleeds. It is not an uncommon condition among swimmers and many have their noses cauterized early but for some reason I did not. A couple of months might go by when I didn't have a nose bleed at all and then they would start one after the other – sometimes so badly that my nose would bleed non-stop for three hours. The only way it could be stopped was by holding my nose and waiting. Almost anything that raised my blood pressure, even slightly, would bring it on. Sometimes it could be something as innocuous as slightly too high water temperature, the exertion of training often aggravated it, as did any little excitement. It was not something that I found particularly worrying and I never exaggerated it in my mind into a more serious condition than it really was but I was annoyed by it. Having constant nose bleeds was a niggly, irritating problem. It kept me out of the pool when I should have been training and it was messy: no one likes being fussed over while blood is spraying everywhere.

We went to see a doctor about it, of course, but he just confirmed that it was a problem many children suffered from and he recommended cauterization if it became any worse. I wasn't enthusiastic about the idea so I never had it cauterized but I do remember that I was particularly bothered by nose bleeds during those Green Shield training sessions. Eventually the problem just fizzled out and after my sixteenth birthday I was hardly affected by them at all but in the four years from twelve onwards a great many swimming pools had a considerable amount of Sharron Davies's blood mixing with their water and chlorine.

Another problem common to swimmers, and to which I fell victim, was ear infections. Water becomes lodged in the ears and, chlorinated or not, an infection, and often a very painful infection, is all too frequently the result. To avoid this I always wore little rubber ear-plugs whenever I was swimming but I was very unlucky:

I started to catch infections from the plugs themselves! The other common ailments of swimmers associated with chlorine I was fortunately spared. Many suffered badly from skin, eye and hair problems – some even gave up swimming because of them – but, apart from nose and ears, I was relatively free of the worst symptoms of swimitis – certainly I never suffered badly enough to make me think of giving up. There were times, however, when my ears caused more than their fair share of worry. Sometimes the infections were so bad I had to visit an Ear, Nose and Throat specialist in Plymouth. He would paint my ears inside and out with some revolting Gentian Violet powder and then pack the ears with wax. What I was not to do under any circumstances was to allow my ears to become wet. This, he said, would counteract any benefit his treatment was having. So what are you to do when you are a swimmer and you cannot get your ears wet? It was a question my father and I pondered for some time until he hit on a solution. He used to stick cotton wool and sticky tape all around my ears until I couldn't hear a thing. Over all this would go a swimming hat and I went into the pool looking like a Martian with great bulges where the ears should have been. It was not very flattering to the vanity but it did allow me to continue training, and for that I was grateful.

Just before the European Championships which were held in August, I upset the training schedule, however, with a typical Sharron injury. Although I was obviously primarily a swimmer, I had not given up other sports. I used to play netball and hockey for my school and I was very keen on athletics. In fact, I used to join in any sport I could. PE was always my favourite lesson and I was considered to be '*tres sportif*'.

However, if there was any mishap that could occur I was usually the one who found it. On this particular occasion I was running in a 100 metres race on the track and, because the track had not been checked and because I am me I caught my foot in a hole not far from the finishing tape. I was running my fastest but my foot became firmly lodged in the hole and the only thing my body could do was to give way at the knee. It did so with searing pain and I tore all the muscles and ligaments in the knee joint. Everything underneath the knee-cap proper was just torn to pieces. My father was white with rage. While I was lying prostrate on the ground totally unable to walk, he was storming around threatening to sue the teacher for negligence. He didn't go ahead with it of course but in the instant of the injury all he could see was his painstaking effort going up in smoke and he was naturally furious.

At the time we never really understood quite how serious that injury was but it did have some beneficial effect. Just as with previous injuries it forced me to build up my arms – still the weakest part of my swimming action. For three weeks I couldn't walk at all and had to be carried everywhere. My knee swelled up like a balloon and whatever training I was able to manage had to be done while sitting or lying down.

For eight weeks while the knee repaired I had physiotherapy every day and ice packs every hour but I also did isokinetic exercises, and it was these that made all the difference.

The previous year Dad had bought the isokinetic swim bench in the United States. It was, in effect, a device to allow a swimmer to swim without being in the water. The bench was a machine that was attached to each limb. It enabled me to swim the four basic racing strokes while, at the same time, regulating the poundage for all sorts of push exercises. I was, for instance, able to push 250 pounds on my back – a weight which would never be safe to try in normal weight training – and it helped me develop the great strength so important for take-off and turning. Eight weeks of non-stop isokinetics – and arm-training in the pool had me almost bursting out of my shoulders. Of course I couldn't use the machine completely as I didn't have the use of my legs. These were strapped down and the machine was used for arms only; making the accident a blessing in disguise. It made me build my arms up and, who knows, it may have been responsible for the wins and laurels that were to come.

Those eight weeks seemed very long and tedious and, perhaps for the first time, I began to think about why I was swimming. That year, 1977, was my option year at school and I was forced to think not only about shaving seconds off my times but also about my future. I was still attending Plymstock Comprehensive but I was quite academic and I was in the top sets for all my subjects. I was

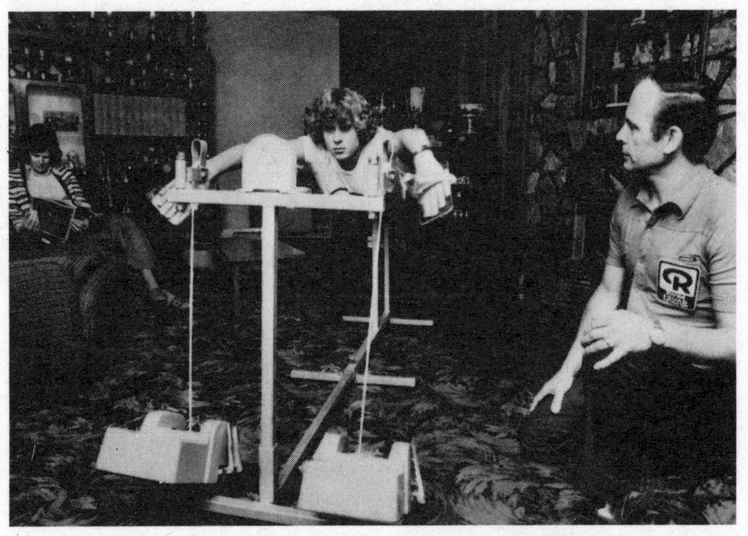

Isokinetic exercises in the lounge every lunchtime under Dad's watchful eye. Mum is sitting in the background, surrounded by my trophies
Associated Newspapers

expected to stay in these sets and sit eight or nine 'O' levels and I wanted to do that too – but I couldn't devote enough time to it and I began to be beset by doubts. I had always known deep inside that Life After Swimming was more important than the swimming itself. Swimming can be a tiny fraction of one's life only but what about my life afterwards? I suddenly began to realize that swimming was preventing me from obtaining the qualifications that would allow me to make the most of my post-swimming life.

Added to this I was now at an age when my classmates were starting to talk about boyfriends and parties and going out to enjoy themselves in the evenings. Until that time no one had really thought about such things. We had just been children and the seeds of independence had not begun to sprout. When they do, of course, the shoots grow very quickly and I found myself resentful and jealous when my friends started going to parties while I was training. I used to be invited to parties and discos but I wasn't allowed to go and, fairly soon, people just didn't bother to invite me. I still had friends at school and I was still quite popular but I was unable to join in any after school activities – it even reached the stage where I couldn't even play hockey or netball for the school because the increasing demands of training did not allow the time.

Now when I look back I realize I wasn't really missing very much. The parties were not that great and I have more opportunities to enjoy them now than I ever would have then – but that was no consolation to me then. I began to resent the never-ending training and I started to pine desperately for a boyfriend and the normal life my friends were leading. The most minor incidents would upset me. During the morning break my friends would often babble on about the film or television programme they had watched the night before. I could never join in because I had never seen what they were talking about.

Although I felt these pressures deeply that stem from a girl growing up it would be wrong for me to give the impression that I thought of abandoning swimming. It was still my life and I had, stronger than ever, high hopes of doing well in the next Olympic Games. That prospect was a fantastic impetus and I wasn't going to allow anything to come in the way of winning a medal. There was a hormonal turmoil going on within my body and I was anxious about my school work and my future prospects but the brightest light and the strongest attraction for me was an Olympic medal and that priority always remained. Sometimes, it is true, it was pushed to the back of my mind and sometimes the adolescent anxieties became almost overpowering but, with my father's help, I managed to keep my eye firmly fixed on that medal and it, more than anything else, saw me through what was a very difficult period.

Being totally truthful I have to say that another factor that kept me going was my growing reputation. I was winning major medals and beginning to experience some of the benefits. I still had to train just as hard – harder perhaps – but it was made easier. Instead of having to train in a pool full of recreational swimmers and screaming kids the council cordoned off two lanes for my exclusive use. It had never done this for any swimmer before but I was bringing the city some prestige and the City Fathers bent over backwards to be helpful. As I have said before this sort of treatment was never allowed to go to my head but I was gratified by it and the recognition and respect that it signified was an encouragement to me. I came to realize that I wasn't just swimming for personal glory and my father, I was swimming for the people of Plymouth as well; I could not let them down.

All this, of course, made it that much more difficult when I injured my knee. The European Championships – a competition at which I was determined to perform well – were only a matter of months away and it seemed likely that I wasn't going to be able to compete. It was probably the importance of this competition that caused both Dad and I to pretend the injury wasn't very serious – at least in the first few hours immediately afterwards. The very next day after the accident my father drove me 200 miles to a competition in Gloucester determined that I was going to swim. He was very angry with me and blamed me for having run in the first place and he was adamant that it wasn't going to upset my training. To be fair to him he didn't really believe I had suffered a serious injury – neither did I for that matter. I was quite a robust girl and we both thought I had just sprained the leg and that the gravity-less exercises that swimming affords would be good for it. Of course it wasn't and

I was unable to get into the pool let alone swim. Poor Dad was beside himself with fury. Not only had I thwarted his training programme but I had also caused him to drive a 400-mile-round trip for nothing.

On top of all that the guesthouse we had booked into for this particular competition turned out to be a brothel. I didn't know what it was; I was still terribly naive, but Dad realized straight away and he worked himself into another rage as he threw together all our belongings and rushed us into the night to look for another place to stay. The whole weekend was a total disaster and both Dad and I wished we could erase it from our minds and start afresh.

Once the leg was healed and I was back in full training the only major competition I could use as a build-up to the European Championships was the Tilt Meet in Paris. This was a fun competition that attracted good swimmers from all over the world and I was optimistic of good performances to confirm my international ranking. I met those times all right but I also had my first hangover!

The accommodation arrangements at the hotel were ripe for mischief. I arrived in Paris with the team and was given a bedroom to share with another girl. In the next room along the corridor were a couple of the boys and the two rooms were separated by a bathroom that had access from both bedrooms. The team management were aghast and the manager, Gerry Thane, made us promise faithfully that we wouldn't venture into each other's rooms. For some reason it did not occur to him to take the obvious course and move us to other rooms: all he did was put us on oath to behave. Of course he was asking for trouble. In order to minimize the ghastly prospect of shower cohabitation between girls and boys Gerry had ruled that the girls could use the shower but the boys could not; but he left us with the keys to the inter-connecting doors. The result was predictable. We didn't pay any attention to the rules and the doors were left open all the time. Technically we were in the clear as the rule in swimming is that no girls are allowed in boys' rooms and vice versa. As we met each other on the neutral ground of the bathroom we were not breaking the rules – but it would have caused something akin to epilepsy if the management had found out. One of the boys did break the rule completely and he came into our room to sleep on the floor. Apparently his bed was very uncomfortable and he could not sleep because the other boy in the room snored too loudly. So in order to get some sleep he brought his pillow and blankets into our room and slept on the carpet. If the officials had discovered him he would probably have been slung out of the team. The fact that he was only 14 would not have made any difference. Rules were rules and swimming officials have never been noted for either a sense of humour or any degree of flexibility.

My first introduction to drinking was through a very silly swimmers' game called Thumper. At the party after the Tilt Meet we played this game with disastrous results. To play it you had to sit on the floor with your legs crossed and pretend to be animals. Each animal had a different hand sign and the game was that, in order, each person would thump on the floor and make the sign for the animal that came next: a sort of memory test. If you made a mistake you had to down a drink in one go. I don't remember a great deal about it and I obviously couldn't remember too many of the animals because I ended up with enough alcohol to dissolve a Breathalyzer bag; miles over the limit and very sorry the next day!

Another build-up meet before the Jönköping European Championships was at Barcelona in Spain and my chief memories of this relate to the general feeling of dirt and decay about the city. I had been looking forward to going to Spain but when I got there I was very disappointed. The city was dirty and the swimming pool was green. There was actually moss growing on the sides of it and it was impossible to see the bottom. It was the worst competition pool I had ever seen (I have still never seen one as filthy) and I found it quite offensive. To make matters worse I disliked the Spanish food. I was off red meat by this time and unused to their cooking methods of hardly cooking meat (I could hardly look at it let alone eat it) and the mashed potato that they served was so watery and insipid it was served in jugs. So I took to eating bread rolls and I would store these in my room by the basketful. As well as supplying basic nutrition they also served as ammunition to lob at the dozens of wild cats that littered the roof-tops outside my window. On many afternoons, to relieve the boredom, we would lob rolls at the cats, scoring points for how many we could hit. Not a very charming occupation and by the time we left it was hardly possible to see those roofs for soggy bread.

Despite the disgusting pool I still won. It was a European Schools Competition and I won about five (I can't remember now exactly how many!) gold medals: so from a morale point of view it was an encouraging build-up for the big test in Sweden still to come.

Although still only 14 I had been an international for more than a year by 1977 and I began to be affected by post-competition depression. I was living on adrenalin. I literally lived for the competition. I would dread the competition but, when it came, would love every minute. I would become totally immersed in it and generate gallons of adrenalin as I applied my whole mind to the task of winning. When it was all over, however, there was nothing – just a feeling of great emptiness with nothing to look forward to. It was this that was hardest. The competition was fun (for there is excitement, perhaps the only true excitement, in being scared stiff – I always was before a race) but the emptiness was depressing. All that lies ahead is day after day of training without any immediate prospect of gratifying competition. The races had become almost like a drug. I missed the stimulus and thrill of competition and the winter periods, when competitions were few, were purgatory.

The big adrenalin boost for 1977 was unquestionably the European Championships. This was my highest target and my most important test. Obviously it wasn't as important a competition as the Olympics but it was the first time I felt I had the opportunity of winning a medal in a major international meeting and against the top Communist country swimmers. Jönköping was where I would prove to myself and to the world my true position in world rankings and the prospect of such a major test petrified me.

Just travelling to Sweden was exciting. I had heard so much about it that I was really looking forward to going and, unlike Spain, I was not disappointed. I was surprised, however, as I was not prepared for the uninhibited Swedish lifestyle. I found their more informal and relaxed attitude to sex, which was clearly visible in their swimming team, quite shocking. I was still very young and at home such matters were never discussed. We all found the idea of men and women sitting around in the nude at the saunas we visited, highly amusing and daring.

I think the sexual freedom of the Swedes rather affected some of the boys in the team and it led to mischief. The diving pit at Jönköping was at the end of the 50-metre pool and there was a glass wall that looked into the diving pool. This was too much for our boys and they took to doing 'moonies' – downing their swimming costumes and pressing their bare backsides against the glass. Six of them used to line up along the diving pool window for the show. It was no more than an adolescent prank but East European officials have even less of a sense of humour than our own and there were countless complaints about the row of white English bottoms that occasionally graced the diving pit view.

For some reason still unclear to me our boys were reprimanded quite mildly – perhaps because it was Sweden after all – but they did get into trouble, quite serious trouble, for trying to steal a Swedish flag. Whenever swimmers visit a foreign country they like to take home a flag as a souvenir, but the Swedes did not appreciate this sentiment. The Swedish police caught some English boys up a flagpole trying to take down a flag and they immediately arrested the offenders. There was even some talk of the boys being thrown in prison and the team management had to act very quickly to stop the Swedish police from bringing out the charge book.

The thing that I found most striking when I was at Jönköping, however – apart from the open-mindedness – was the impoverished nature of the East European, and particularly the Russian, teams. At international competitions there is always trading between teams. Competitors liked to swap swimming costumes and bits and pieces so that they would have lifelong souvenirs of the event. The Russians had nothing to trade: at least nothing in which a 14-year-old would be interested. We had quite a trendy physiotherapist called Tony at the time and he was in his element swapping oddments of gear for vodka and caviar (which the Russians seemed to possess in bulk) but he was unable to find a costume or personal nick nack which he could prize as a souvenir. The Russians, it seemed, would do almost anything to lay their hands on Tony's home-made massage concoctions and they were only too happy to give him their alcohol and fish eggs for it.

But for some bureaucratic reason known only to themselves the Russian swimmers were not allowed to swap their costumes. I managed to exchange one of my costumes for a large Russian doll but I could not obtain a costume for love nor money: and I tried because costumes are the most prized souvenirs of all. I came to feel terribly sorry for the Russian and East German girls and I ended up giving one of my costumes away for nothing to an East German girl who was really desperate to have it.

As I have already mentioned, it was steroids first and second in the race and Sharron Davies third. It was the best result I could have hoped for and it shot me even further into the limelight as far as the press was concerned. I held a press conference, which was very emotional, for the first time in my life. The serious swimming press started to pay me attention and I began to be on first-name terms with some of the great names of Fleet Street. Photographs of me crying with emotion and relief when the Union Jack was hoisted up at the medal ceremony appeared in virtually every newspaper in Britain and I became, almost overnight, one of Fleet Street's favourite young ladies. It all helped to make me feel very proud. I knew, and the press realized too, that if it wasn't for the East German steroids I would have won an even better medal – possibly the gold – and I was treated more like the champion than the bronze medal winner. It put greater pressure on me, of course, as some commentators were now openly naming me as a Moscow medal prospect and I knew it would be more difficult staying at the top than it had been reaching it.

In addition to that bronze medal, however, I received a very nice Jönköping bonus; a bronze medal in the relay. This was totally unexpected and came about because three of the other teams were disqualified. The Swedish authorities had installed pad-controlled take-overs on the starting blocks. The swimmer on the block was not allowed to leave the block until the swimmer in the pool had touched it. She could be moving but her feet must still be in contact until the touch. Until then if the swimmer on the block left with a splashy movement as the swimmer coming in touched it was difficult to tell exactly whether the rules had been met. But at Jönköping they had also installed devices that indicated when the feet actually left the diving block. There was electronic co-ordination between the touch and foot pads and three of the teams started too early and were disqualified by the electronic devices. All three of those teams, the West Germans, the Dutch and the Swedish girls, would probably have beaten us but their expulsion enabled us to capture the bronze medal and I was delighted to be taking two medals home to Plymouth instead of just the one that I had been half expecting to win.

When I arrived back in England I could not have been happier. I had more than met my target for the year and I had given myself the boost that I needed in order to overcome some of the creeping adolescent doubts. I now began to think hungrily about the 1978 Commonwealth Games at Edmonton in Canada and I knew that an eventual Olympic medal was much more than a schoolgirl's fantasy.

CHAPTER FIVE

Edmonton

One journalist at the 1977 European Championships was moved to
write in his paper that I had 'blossomed' into a young woman while
at the Championships. To him I had left a girl and come back a
young woman. In some ways I suppose he was right. Not only was
the Jönköping bronze my swimming coming of age but the time
spent in the village produced my first proper boyfriend. In the
period of a week or so I developed a teenage crush on West German
European butterfly champion Michael Kraus. Together we went
to a fireworks display and a disco. I admit that this doesn't sound
much like the behaviour of someone who had just blossomed into
womanhood but it was a major step towards growing up for me. I
had never really been one for swimming boyfriends. There had
been plenty of one-evening romances but I had never had a crush
on anyone and I had never actively pursued a boy. But with Michael
I was completely bowled over and I wanted to be wherever he was
all the time. It never got past the pecking stage – I was after all still
only 14 (Michael was 20!) and very definitely a 'nice girl'. I will
always remember him; I suppose for a couple of weeks I was really
in love, the sort of all consuming love only a teenager can manage,
and it affected the rest of my life. Certainly I felt much more worldly
wise when I returned to England.

What it also meant, of course, was that my usual post competition
blues were even more acute. As well as missing the adrenalin of
competition I was also pining for my new love and my father had a
tough job persuading me to throw myself back into my training.
Eventually I did, probably because training was habitual and
indulgence in habits can be good therapy.

The first competition after Jönköping was the National Age

Group Championships which were held in Blackpool. They were the last Age Groups I entered because it was becoming pointless competing against kids when my only real rivals were in the senior grades. Needless to say I won my races easily enough but I remember that Blackpool meet for something outside of the pool. It was the first time I met a 15-year-old by the name of Alison Love. Alison was the daughter of the owners of the guesthouse in which we were staying. I don't know whether my father noticed her much then but she was later to play a very large part in all our lives. Blackpool was the first occasion I had met Alison and it will always be memorable as the beginning of a bizarre series of events.

An added note of irony stems from the fact that my mother and brothers also came on that trip to Blackpool. They hadn't had a holiday for years and had been domiciled in Plymouth for most of the time that Dad and I were trotting around the world. It was quite a treat for them to join us on this occasion: but it turned into a nightmare for my mother, both in the long and short term. The long term we will come to later – the nature of its destructiveness needs more time and space to develop – but the short-term disaster seemed no less distressing at the time. After months of seeing nothing of us, Mum came to Blackpool for a holiday and spent the entire time in bed with a gall bladder problem. She had to be rushed to hospital for an operation and I am sure that, for her, that Blackpool holiday is remembered as one of the blackest of her life.

It is only with hindsight, of course, that I can see just how miserable that Blackpool trip must have been. At the time I felt sorry for Mum but I concentrated on the swimming: and it never occurred to me that Alison was anything more than an acquaintance of the family. I was there to swim and I did just that.

Already my reputation was beginning to introduce me to new worlds. Not long after we returned from Jönköping I received a telephone call from the great sports photographer Tony Duffy. He told me he had chosen four female sports personalities and put each of them into different situations for a day-long photographic session. One was to ride bikes, another was to sing, the third was to do a trapeze act and I was to be a model.

I was overjoyed. It was an unusual occurrence – just the remedy for my depression – and I agreed immediately. I was to be a model for a day. Not long afterwards I was picked up and whisked off to Norman Hartnell's. I was made up with the full works and shown how to walk up and down the cat-walk in a way that would show off the dresses I was modelling. It was slightly daunting for me as Hartnell's is such a famous salon and I was sure that I wouldn't do things correctly – but I needn't have worried. As I was walking up and down wearing a very floaty, chiffon dress, a large woman dressed all in pink in the audience announced, with rather a large plum in her mouth, 'How lovely, darling, Norman order me one of those.' No sooner had she spoken than she waltzed out but I was absolutely delighted. I must have been satisfactory as a model as I had sold a dress. Tony was pleased too because he took some good photographs and Norman Hartnell received good publicity as well as a sale. It was a very successful day and great fun.

At the end of 1977 it was decision-time again in the Davies family. My father resolved to give up his insurance business to become a full-time coach. It was an inevitable decision as swimming had gradually absorbed more and more of his time and his business partners were understandably annoyed at his lack of contribution. He would probably have given it up earlier had he been able to find another source of income. This had proved difficult but the end of 1977 saw the completion of a sponsorship deal with Rollei. The West German camera company were to pay for my father to coach his group of Plymouth swimmers. It meant that he could now devote the whole of his time to the squad, and me in particular, and it meant that he no longer had to go through the motions of working for the insurance business. Before this time my father's life had been dominated by swimming perhaps 90 per cent of the time; now he was completely immersed in it and it made training just that little bit tougher for me. My father was one to take his responsibilities seriously and, now that he was a professional coach with pro-fessional challenges, he set about training me with renewed vigour. And for my part I wanted, more than ever, to do well for my father the 'pro' coach.

Because I had won a medal at the European Championships at Jönköping I was promoted from the Green Shield junior squad into the senior Yorkshire Bank squad for Christmas training. Like the Green Shield squad, training was held at Crystal Palace during the school holidays but we had to work that much harder and I revelled in the promotion. The track and field athletes were also in training at Crystal Palace at the time and I met Daley Thompson for the first time. He rushed up to a friend and me and more or less demanded a T-shirt my friend was wearing. There was nothing backward about Daley and, though I liked him, I had no idea how well I would get to know him later.

There was still much swimming and training to be done before Edmonton: some of it, strangely enough, in Canada. At the end of 1977 my father and I went to Etobicoke in Toronto under Rollei sponsorship. This was a very important trip and perhaps the single most important coaching session of my life. My father had decided that, as I was going to compete in Canada in 1978 at the Commonwealth Games, I should obtain some first-hand knowledge of local conditions and watch some of the Canadian girls who were likely to be my most serious challengers. In addition a former Great Britain coach called Derek Snelling was in Canada at that time, for whom my father had the greatest respect. Derek had written to my father to say he would very much like us to go and train with them. Armed with this invitation, my father asked Rollei to pay our expenses to go to Toronto for New Year training. We were prepared to work hard and we were prepared to learn – what we had not envisaged was the bitter Canadian winter. Leaving the aeroplane was like entering the freezer compartment of a refrigerator. Snow was everywhere, as high as my ears if I strayed off the cleared paths, and I don't think I had ever felt so cold in my life. But cold or not I found it wonderful and quite romantic. I wasn't too upset either when we kept getting snowed in and I didn't have to go to training sessions – it was a welcome relief as the training sessions were the hardest I had ever experienced. They were crazy; if I wasn't in the water swimming I was below weight training. Derek was a hard taskmaster.

The conditions and facilities were fabulous. The pool was light and inviting to swim in and all the other facilities, such as the weight room, were in the same building. It meant that when we were not snowed in we could spend all of our time in the pool, doing weight training. All that we needed was there – quite a contrast to Plymouth where the facilities were Stone Age in comparison. The Canadians even had a full-time medical centre under the pool; a sensible idea but unheard of in England.

The original plan had been for us to have a two-week trip to Etobicoke but Derek Snelling devised a training system that required one hard week, one medium week and one easy week.

Somehow we were going to have to make arrangements to stay another week, not only because the training was going so well but also because there were a couple of competitions that I wanted to enter which took place after we were due to leave. We needed a week's extension on our airline tickets but the airline would not hear of it. As far as they were concerned it was a charter ticket and not extendable. It put us in a quandary. We had to stay but we could not afford to buy new tickets. The only answer was dishonesty. We decided my father had to be ill; the small print on the ticket having revealed that we could extend the time of the ticket if certified unfit to travel by a doctor. It didn't prove too difficult to find a sympathetic doctor prepared to sign the sick note for the extra week. It worked perfectly and everyone was happy – even the airline.

The trip was a complete success. The pool, the people, the training and the races far exceeded all expectations; even my diet improved. As well as refining the actual swimming technique, Derek Snelling also liked to concentrate on diet and nutrition. Because of this I had to undergo medical, fitness and stress tests. In the process nine test tubes of blood were taken from my arm (I thought they were taking so much I would have none left) and it was discovered that I was lacking in calcium and iron. This was because I refused to eat red meat and my protein intake was too low. The result was that I had to start taking brewers' yeast tablets every day and drink a disgusting whisked-up witches' brew of raw eggs and Complan every morning before I went swimming. I hated it. I had never been one to be fussed over and I nearly rebelled against these over-elaborate, in my view anyway, dietary tortures. But though I was against it my father thought it was a good idea and so that was that; it was eggs, Complan and brewers' yeast or nothing. I took the easy way out, even though I seemed to rattle every time I dived into the pool.

I will always be grateful to Derek, despite his insistence on the foul concoctions, because he made me realize the value of stretching. Until then I had done strength exercises but I had tackled very little flexibility. Derek changed all that and he introduced me to a complete flexibility programme which I still use today. The visit would have been worthwhile for the flexibility alone but the trip also helped to revive my interest in swimming.

Short courses are always used for winter training and the Canadians – being an ingenious people – had developed a boom system that created two 25-metre pools out of their Olympic pool. I trained in this shortened pool and it was used for the two competitions in the last week. In one of these I competed against the Canadian National Champion and World record holder Nancy Garapick. I didn't beat her only, I also broke 36 British and English junior and senior records. It was a purple patch for me and I was really eating up the work. I had a genuine appetite for swimming again and my desire for a world medal was as strong, if not stronger, as it had ever been. Canada helped me to fall in love with swimming again. Because of that wonderful trip – plus the memories of Montreal and Edmonton – Canada is, next to Britain, my favourite country.

The only disadvantage of winning so well at Toronto was that I had to carry six huge marble trophies home with me on the aeroplane. They were not an onerous burden but the customs officers gave me a sideways glance at Heathrow: I think they thought I looked suspicious and I thought for a while they were not going to allow me to pass. Still they were worth the trouble and they look very handsome in the trophy cabinet at home in Plymouth.

Hardly had I arrived back in Britain than I was leaving again: this time with the British team for an international in Rhode Island. The swimming itself was not very memorable and I can remember little about it. What I do remember, however, is a training trip, immediately afterwards, to Nashville in the Deep South. It was like dreamland for me. Although not a fan of country music, I adored visiting places like the Grand Old Opry and the Hall of Fame. I must have taken more photographs of Elvis Presley's gold

Cadillac than of anything else since I left Britain. I went quite berserk with the camera and seemed to be snapping at everything I saw. I must have spent a small fortune on buying film but those pictures are now among my most treasured souvenirs.

Nashville may have been a dream but coming back to England turned into a marathon nightmare. We were booked on a direct flight from Nashville to London – normally an eight-hour flight – but found ourselves circling over Heathrow for three hours because of fog. Eventually it was decided that a London landing was impossible so we were diverted to Amsterdam where we spent six hours waiting for the London weather to clear. Being London, of course, it failed to oblige and it was decided that we should be taken to a hotel, fed, and put to bed for the night. We were told that they would call us in the morning and they did – 1 a.m.! Still heavy with sleep we were taken back to the airport by bus where we were told our aeroplane was ready to take off. Needless to say it wasn't. Instead of being cosily tucked up in the hotel bed we had to pace the departure lounge floor for another six hours. When we finally set foot on English soil again it was two full days after leaving the United States. It was easily my worst travel experience and I was completely exhausted. Once back in Plymouth I think I slept for 24 hours non-stop; an unheard of luxury.

Although this was 1978 and a Commonwealth Games year, my thoughts were very much on school and I felt very honoured when, in April, I was invited to open a new indoor swimming pool at Kelly College near Tavistock and was also offered an athletic scholarship to the College starting in September, following the Games. An added bonus was that my father was also offered a position at the school as head coach and so we both had much on our minds as we drove away from the College after the pool opening. It was a marvellous opportunity for both of us, but such a fundamental change in our lives, that we couldn't bring ourselves to make a decision straight away. We knew it was a heaven-sent opportunity – an offer that we could not refuse – but the implications were so enormous that, for the first few weeks afterwards, we could hardly bring ourselves to talk about it. Anyway, the priority was preparing for Edmonton.

Once again we started to cram in as many competitions as possible to sharpen up my speed and once again I went to the Tilt Meet in Paris – where I was more than pleased to see the family who had put me up on my very first trip abroad more than five years earlier. They still couldn't speak any English and I still spoke no French but we hugged and kissed and it was very touching that they had taken the trouble to drive some distance just to come and see me. At that meeting I swam for them – I always liked to swim for someone other than myself (usually it was my father) – and captured a couple more British records. Having someone else to swim for and hearing supporters yelling in the crowd has always been important for me, and now that I was becoming known as a world-ranking swimmer who was expected to win I relied on this outside help even more. Fame has its rewards and I was enjoying my share of them: I never felt uneasy in the limelight but I had to spend more and more lonely hours training to remain in it. Hearing supporters cheering for me made those weeks of mindless slog worthwhile and I am sure my times were always that extra bit faster when I was aware of that support spurring me on. It is hard to know and impossible to prove but I wouldn't be at all surprised if the support of those French friends drove me a good 0·5 faster at the Tilt.

In England the two big tests before Edmonton were the National Short Course and the National Long Course Championships. The Short Course, still technically part of the winter training, was valuable more as a training exercise than as an assault on gold medals. Even so I came away from that competition with five golds – in fact, a win in every event I entered. Naturally I was elated. I had bettered the Edmonton qualifying time as well as winning and that was important; indeed it was more important than winning because my opposition was not very strong.

Satisfactory though the Short Course Championships proved, I knew it was the more prestigious Long Course competition that was going to make or break me for the Commonwealth Games. It wasn't any good just attending and winning the medleys. To ensure my place, I wanted to show the selectors that I was the fastest in the country in the individual strokes as well. To win a place in the team I had to be in the first two but I was determined to go as number

In the lounge at home after winning seven national titles and gold
medals at the National Long Course Championships in 1978

one and I took my preparation for the 1978 National Long Course as seriously as I had trained for anything before. I was expecting to do well and when the Championships came around I knew I was fast and fit but I was surprised at the degree to which I was dominant.

At the end of that competition seven gold medals were hanging around my neck. It was unprecedented. No one had taken as many national titles before and I found myself splashed across the sporting pages of every paper in the country.

In all the disciplines apart from the breaststroke, it seemed that I only had to swim to win. I won the 200 backstroke, the 100, 200, 400 and 800 metres front-crawl, and the 200 and 400 individual medleys. These races were swum over a period of three days and I couldn't possibly have entered any more. I probably would have won medals in other events had I competed but I was swimming three times a day and I had heats and finals so there simply was not time to pack in anything else.

The press, predictably, had a field day. No one had ever won seven titles at a national championships before. I was given a special award by the press for being the star personality and my father and I seemed to be under siege as reporter after reporter harried us with a never-ending torrent of questions. All were full of praise and wonder at my achievement and they all wrote about how exhausted I was by it all. I was understandably shattered but the press made much of it. Even John Hennessy, *The Times'* reporter not usually given to hyperbole, said I was completely washed out after the 200 backstroke. It is true that I had 25 minutes to spare only after the end of the 200 metres freestyle (in which I made a huge surge at the end to beat reigning record holder Cheryl Brazendale by a yard) to the start of the backstroke final, and it is also true that I left it until the last 100 to make my final spurt but it wasn't my hardest race by any means. If I looked excessively exhausted to the press at the end of it, it was probably because they had raced that last length with me and felt exhausted themselves: I have seen reporters more winded than athletes at the end of exciting races on many occasions.

I was, naturally, delighted but it was not my biggest achievement. Dad was absolutely thrilled, for me mostly, of course, but also because, now that he was a professional coach, it was a big feather in his professional cap. I got a big kick just from seeing his face when I won. At the press conferences he played it down slightly by saying that the ultimate goal was the 1980 Moscow Olympics and any successes along the way were just a bonus. Basically that was true. I was aiming primarily at a Moscow medley medal but those seven national titles were still very precious to us; bonus or not.

Another bonus is that I really cannot envisage anyone overtaking that seven-title record. Not because Britain lacks top-quality swimmers now but quite the reverse. British swimming has improved vastly in recent years so that the competitors now have to specialize much more in one or two events than I had to do. I hit my form when British swimming was at a low ebb and I took a record that was for the taking. The added pressures of swimming in the 1980s have really made it impossible for the record to be challenged again. Of course I may be mistaken and there may be someone, somewhere, with no other goal in view than to take eight national titles in one go. In which case, good luck to her, she will need it.

Now that I was virtually unchallenged at the top of women's swimming I had to keep my eyes open, not only for lurking news reporters but also for other swimmers. Since our return from Toronto with all the new fangled ideas, every man and his dog in the swimming world wanted to share them. Everyone was interested in my new stretching exercises and in my pre-race diet of melons filled with glucose. It was as if they all thought that a stretch and a melon would somehow give them a share of my success. In reality, of course, the only way to get there is still by spending years grinding away and piling up the mileage in a swimming pool – melons and glucose help but the only vehicle with sufficient power to make the climb to the top is single-minded dedication. I had driven myself remorselessly, with the help of many vigorous hands and the constant coaxing of my father, for over six years. I had eaten and slept swimming for nearly as long as I could remember and, only now, was I reaping the benefits of that work. It may have seemed like overnight success to some of the press and to some of my rivals but for me it was the beginning of the wins that I had spent most of my life striving for: and it was a reward I felt I deserved – I had waited a long time.

Important though those Championships were, and crucial as they were for the now imminent Commonwealth Games, my main concern and fiercest struggles were in the classroom, not the swimming pool. 'O' levels were in full swing and I was working as hard as I could at Plymstock Comprehensive. I still hadn't fully made up my mind whether to take the offer of the Kelly College scholarship but I was determined to do as well in the exams as I was able because I was anxious to have something to fall back on when my swimming career had to end. It was important to me that I didn't allow medals to obscure my view of the future.

Falling plump in the middle of 'O' level studies, however, were the Edmonton Games themselves and, for their duration at least, I gave my attention 100 per cent to swimming again. I was going in the expectation of bringing back more than one medal and I settled back into training with the extra verve that only swimming for your country can give. One thing I had to do first, though, was go to see my doctor about being given the pill. I found it a terribly embarrassing experience, especially as I didn't want it for its more usual purpose – rather I needed it for a far more mundane reason. Female swimmers need the pill to help control their periods. It is impossible to explain the degree to which periods can upset the equilibrium and general tone of female swimmers and the pill is needed so that periods are as regular as possible. I suffered more than most with period pains and this often put me off colour for training and the pill would keep my monthly cycle as stable as possible. The necessity of it didn't stop me blushing bright puce when I asked the doctor for it, however.

Training for the Commonwealth Games was held at York, the first time a camp had been taken away from Crystal Palace. It was a ridiculous decision. The York pool was a small college pool and not adequate for the requirements of a national squad in full training. On top of that there simply wasn't enough room. When a large number of swimmers are bashing around in a small pool the chlorine is shaken and it rises into the air. At York there was not enough air space in the building for the chlorine to disperse and many of the team suffered from chlorine poisoning. They gave us the pool because it was available all day every day if we so wished but it just wasn't up to the high standards a British team demands. We didn't even have the basic modern conveniences we had come to expect from Crystal Palace and there was dissent in the camp. It wasn't that the masses were revolting – far from it, we were far too excited about where we were going for that – but there were grumbles. I think, underneath, most of us felt we deserved better.

On 21 July 1978 we left Heathrow for Canada amid the sort of departure chaos that was becoming quite commonplace to me. Fortunately, this time we had been issued with proper uniforms which no one felt embarrassed about wearing. I had been to Canada several times before and I had suffered, and enjoyed, the press ballyhoo that accompanies the departure of national teams. I suppose I was becoming just a little blasé about it all and I accepted it, at least as far as the rest of the world was concerned, with a shrug of the shoulders. Inside I was just as excited as anyone else – perhaps more so as I was carrying the added responsibility of being a 'medal prospect' – but I was something of a veteran now (at 15!) and it wouldn't have been very impressive for me to let the new team members see me looking too wide-eyed.

I can't beat about the bush too much about Edmonton. It was simply the very best international competition of the whole of my career. They called it the Friendly Games and it was just that. Everyone was together. The security, though still very much in evidence, was not as tight or as restricting as at the Olympic Games, and there was definitely a feeling that we were all from one united family of nations. There was still intense patriotism, of course, and there was a tendency for some, particularly the Canadians and the Australians, to not only cheer their own but also be derisory of the opposition. At first I was a little annoyed by this but I soon realized it was all part of the game and I used it to fuel my own determination.

Accommodation at Edmonton was as pleasant as Games' villages can be. There were two to a bedroom; I shared with a girl called Heidi Turk, a Gloucester swimmer. Heidi, and her sister Mitzi, had been friends of mine for a very long time. We got on well together and there were no problems sharing; a very important consideration at major games. The village was well laid out, again with men's and women's blocks, and the facilities and dining hall were just as good as they had been at Montreal. Also, the weather was on our side and the sun was blazing down enabling Heidi and me to make full use of our little sunbathing patio. I don't think any of us had a single complaint.

The only disappointment was that I was not allowed to take part in the opening ceremony. Because swimming events are always held at the beginning of the Games I found myself scheduled to compete the day after the ceremony, the first day of actual competition, and under team rules that meant no undue stress or excitement the day before. I don't think for a minute I would have suffered any ill-effects by marching with the team and I hated being forced to watch from the sidelines but, as I have said before, swimming officials do not bend rules. There was no way they were going to make an exception just because Davies wanted to march!

The disappointment of missing the opening, however, was more than compensated for by another incident: I met Daley Thompson again. Just as at Crystal Palace eight months earlier, he marched up, bold as brass, and introduced himself again. I was thrilled to see him and we often saw each other in the village. There was a disco in the camp that went on until ten o'clock at night and we took to going there in the evenings. Even though I was still only 15, many took me for older. It had also been the case at Montreal when I was 13 and even then I had gone out with the odd athlete. I had been friendly with a pole vaulter at Montreal and it now transpired that he was a friend of Daley's. One evening at the disco, Daley introduced me to him and it was as though we had rehearsed it. Neither of us gave the slightest indication that we had met before and we blandly went through the formalities of introduction.

When I say that the disco went on until 10 p.m. I meant that was the time when the swimmers had to leave, in Cinderella fashion, at 10 p.m. The track and field people, generally older and allowed much more freedom anyway, continued cavorting until much later. It meant, of course, that Daley and I didn't have a chance to come to know each other very well. We often went to fairs and other such things while we were in Edmonton. Because the athletes had more freedom and often had access to cars it was not difficult for him to arrange and I remember once going to a fair with him, Tessa Sanderson and Donna Hartley which was great fun. Daley and I enjoyed each other's company and we shared a similar sense of humour but it wasn't a raging romance because we were both in training, and doing well in our respective sports which, after all, was why we were there. Sometimes we went three days without seeing each other because we both had our own things to do. I knew it was the beginning of a romance and I knew that Daley was interested and I was flattered. I had reciprocal feelings for him but it wasn't until after the Games that I really came to know him. He made the effort to come and see me compete which was touching.

In the pool I did my job well and finished the only British swimmer to take a gold. Duncan Goodhew was pipped to the post by Graham Smith of Canada and it was left to me to keep the flag flying. I ended up with two golds, a silver and a bronze – fulfilling even my wildest dreams. I enjoyed winning all of those medals but the sweetest of all was the 400 metres individual medley. In this I beat convincingly Canada's Olympic medallists Becky Smith and Cheryl Gibson in a new British record time of 4:52.44. I was slightly disappointed that I hadn't managed to beat the 4:50 mark (a target I had mentally set myself) but it was my last race and the end of a quite perfect week. I was happy and exhausted.

Indeed tiredness was a problem at these games. When the team first arrived I had intended swimming in more events but I had to change my plans. I didn't swim in the 400 metres freestyle and I pulled out of the final of the 200 metres backstroke. When I got up in the morning my muscles ached badly and I had to spend some time with the physiotherapist before going into the pool. I found it quite worrying because I was not normally prone to such debilitating bouts of tiredness and I rang my father in England several times for advice. He told me to forget about set plans and just to swim. I was to forget about the clock and to try to enjoy the races as races. In the 400 medley I did just that and it was a huge thrill to beat the Canadian girls again but I was glad when it was over. I won that race on 9 August and it was my last event in the Games but I could not allow myself complete relaxation. Only ten days away were the World Championships – a much tougher competition all round and

Just after winning the gold in the 200 metres individual medley at
Edmonton
Allsport

Outside the Heathrow Excelsior, feeling exhausted after the
Commonwealth Games and about to leave for the World
Championships in West Berlin. Mum, Dad and the twins had come up
from Plymouth to see me for the day

I had to try to maintain my form.

However, when that medley was over the weight of those particular games was lifted from me and I was able to go dancing and enjoy myself in Daley's company. Not long after that race it was arranged that I go on the Terry Wogan programme for a chat, but it turned out to be much more than that. Terry had managed to link up a three-way conversation so that I was not only talking to the studio but also to my parents who were in a BBC studio in Plymouth. The programme started with me talking to Terry Wogan and then he introduced my parents to ask for their comments but the conversation began to become a bit out of control. Instead of being a three-way radio interview it took the form of a private telephone call. I started to have a technical conversation with my father and my mother butted in with a 'what are you doing tonight?' When I said I was going out she came back quickly with 'Who with?' As soon as they heard it was Daley Thompson my father butted in with a very pointed and ominous 'Who?'. My mother, like all mothers I suppose, could ask only if I had enough clean clothes and was eating properly. Terry Wogan, of course, was quite beside himself with all this. Perhaps for the first time in his life he found himself not being able to get a word in edgeways. I hadn't seen my parents for about a month and a half and there was so much to gabble about that we completely forgot that Terry was on the line as well. In the end he had to butt in to remind us that we were holding this family conference in BBC time. He took it all in good humour but he has never asked to interview me again to steal his thunder!

Daley was my first real relationship. My friendship with Michael Kraus the year before, had been more in the form of a crush on my part with little coming back from him. Now I was nearly 16 and Daley liked me as much as I liked him. Constant travelling and competing had made me very mature for my age but there was still a part of me which wanted to be rushed off my feet by a gallant Knight and with Daley showing as much interest in me as I felt for him I was in seventh heaven for a while. Daley was really my first love and there is a soft spot in my heart for him still.

Although Daley and I both led separate lives we continued to see each other after the Games. He used to come down to Plymouth to stay with us (my mother liked him from the start and even my father eventually came to like him) and he bought me a lovely gold chain for my sixteenth birthday. We even spent that Christmas together and we both knew that, if I had been living in London, we would have had quite a serious relationship. The press were very interested in our romance and naturally blew it up out of all proportion, some papers even predicting marriage. It made excellent news. The sheer distance between us, however, and the different demands of our respective sports, effectively stopped us from becoming as close as perhaps we would have liked. Daley was quite a major influence on me then. He was, in his private life, nothing like the roustabout that the press sometimes like to paint him. One of his favourite occupations was just to go for long walks and talk. We may have met up in discos but we never stayed there. After a dance or two we would always wander off by ourselves to talk.

Apart from my relationship with Daley the press were now full of my prospects for beating the world. For them it was a matter of first the Commonwealth, next the world. It was, of course, just what I wanted too but when the press, and through them the public, expected such great things of me it formed an enormous pressure that I could well have done without. I was fortunate in that I never found it too difficult to cope with media exposure and I never allowed it to affect the way I thought about myself. Others did not find it so easy. The fuss they made of Cheryl Brazendale when she broke the 60-second barrier for the 100 freestyle, for instance, was nearly the downfall of poor Cheryl. She could have been a really good sprinter if it wasn't for the press. When Cheryl broke that barrier, which a couple of hundred people throughout the world had already done, she was shot from relative obscurity to instant stardom. Lindsay MacDonald, the athlete, was another victim of Fleet Street. Lindsay was good and she was keen but she still had a long way to go. She realized it and the more responsible sports-writers realized it too yet those with an eye for a headline and with-out any thought for the person behind it, started to rave about Lindsay becoming the great British star of the 1980s. It was un-necessary pressure from which she should have been spared. She was too young and too fragile for the newspaper tanks and received a blow to her confidence. I know Lindsay is trying desperately to make a comeback in top athletics and I wish her the very best of luck but if she succeeds again it will be through her own dedication and no thanks to Fleet Street.

Sometimes I think that sportswriters should adopt a more responsible approach. Of course if they recognize a genuinely exciting new talent, then by all means write about him or her; but they should spare a thought about how damaging, in the long term, it can be to the sportsperson concerned to predict Olympic golds or other similar heights. Athletes need time to develop rhythms and have to be able to work at their own pace.

Fortunately I was shielded from some of the worst excesses of the press by my father. He would keep them away from me, by moderate force if necessary. He would tell them when to stop pestering us and he counterbalanced all their predictions of a glittering future by telling me they didn't know what they were talking about and that, in fact, I wasn't that good. It's true I was naturally stronger than some of the other girls, and I may well have withstood the media barrage without Dad, but with him I was impregnable and it was a great advantage.

At the end of that year, 1978, the sportswriters, the same ones I have just been criticizing, elected me their Sportswoman of the Year. I could hardly believe it. I had to attend their gala dinner in London and open the dancing with their Sportsman of the Year – none other than Daley Thompson. Daley and I had had a minor argument just before the dinner and we managed to dance without looking at each other once. It was a waltz but neither of us knew how to waltz so we just smooched around the floor – each trying to pretend that the other didn't exist. It must have looked quite amusing but the photographs that were taken somehow didn't quite capture the atmosphere between us and it was only more fuel for the Daley and Sharron matchmakers.

Despite the disagreement, the dinner was a very proud moment for me but I still managed to ruin my speech. I had planned to say that I accepted the award on behalf of swimming rather than for myself but what I actually said was that Britain had not produced a world-class swimmer since Anita Lonsborough and she had been competing before I was born. Of course I should have chosen my words more carefully. Anita was upset that, within one sentence, I had transformed her into an old woman. She was not very pleased with me for some time afterwards but she is too nice a person to bear a grudge and we are now the best of friends again. It was good experience, however. I don't make such silly mistakes in speeches any more. It's just a shame that Anita should have been the victim of that particular gaffe.

That sportswriters' dinner was my social highlight of the year. I was invited to several other social functions throughout the year but my father never considered them sufficiently important and I was not allowed to go. But even he had to recognize the honour of the Sportswoman of the Year award and it was my passport out of Plymouth – if only for a few days.

The day after the awards Daley and I made it up and he took me on a romantic boat trip down the river. Quite the perfect way to end an almost perfect year. If I had known what was to come, however, I would have tried to wring even more joy from that day . . . 1979 hardly had a moment of happiness at all.

CHAPTER SIX

Kelly College

1979 was my 'O' level year and the year was a disaster. It wasn't that I made a mess of things academically – it was more that all the frustrations and little niggles of my life began to have a cumulative effect and, had it not been for the prospect of the Moscow Olympics, there is a good chance I would have given up my career in swimming.

My father had decided that we should both go to the school. He would accept the coaching position and I was to become a boarder to study for my 'O' levels while training in the school pool. Kelly College was a private school on Dartmoor. It was originally a naval school but by 1979 it was just an ordinary private school, though with naval links, and the original all-boy constitution had been amended so that girls were allowed in the sixth form. The school was not particularly sports orientated but it had built the pool (which I had opened in April 1978), and it was looking for ways to make the pool help the school's finances. The headmaster, Dennis Ball, aware that the school was going through a sticky patch, decided to offer scholarships to some of the better swimmers so that they could reap the benefits of a good pool on their doorstep with a top coach at hand. The scholarships themselves were not cheap. Just because my father was the school coach did not mean that I was taken on as a pupil for nothing. Dennis Ball offered Dad a discount of one-third only and my parents still had to find funds in the region of £2500 a year to keep me at Kelly but it was considered that the advantages outweighed the disadvantages and I took up my boarding position – as the youngest girl that had ever attended the school.

The advantage of Kelly from my parents' point of view was that the masters would be available to teach me at weekends and in the evenings and I wouldn't have to travel to do my training.

In addition, as my father was the coach with the authority to offer scholarships himself, it meant that I would now have the chance to train beside better swimmers. Instead of training with Port of Plymouth where I was in a class of my own, I would train with good swimmers from all over the country – and this is just what happened. An example of how effective it was is shown by the fact that, when the Olympics did come around, my father had four swimmers in the team.

So, for me, it wasn't the swimming that bothered me. At first that couldn't really have been better. But I was not so satisfied with my academic work. By going to Kelly it meant that I had to throw away a whole year of my Plymstock Comprehensive 'O' level course. I had to drop many of the subjects that I enjoyed, such as typing and domestic science, and take on new subjects instead. At Plymstock I had studied human biology but at Kelly I had to switch to ordinary biology which was a totally new subject to me. The physics that I had been taking at Plymstock clashed with Kelly's geography class so physics had to go . . . it went on and on. The end result was that I was taking five 'O' levels at Kelly whereas I had been doing nine at Plymstock; but, paradoxically, the work was harder. In some subjects I was having to make up two years' work in one and that, on top of my swimming, was a very heavy workload. In the end I passed all five exams that I sat and I was obviously delighted.

Then the swimming side, which should have been so wonderful, turned into a nightmare.

Because my father was the coach and he had other internationals in his squad he felt that there was no way he could allow me to dodge anything and he came down on me even harder than usual. It wasn't completely his fault and there were other reasons – my parents were drifting apart for instance – but the two of us started to argue constantly, sometimes quite violently, and a definite rift developed between us. At home there were countless arguments and life was far from rosy. I didn't realize how strained my parents' marriage was though I knew things were far from happy and the tensions that I was feeling came out in the form of intransigence in the swimming pool.

My father, Terry Davies, while coaching at Kelly College
Sporting Pictures

Father–daughter relations were also exacerbated by the fact that I was growing up. I was now 16 but my father continued to treat me as though I was still a little girl. I think probably all fathers have this problem. Certainly my father refused to realize that I was growing up and beginning to think differently. It led to violent rows and sometimes he was quite brutal with me.

With hindsight it was understandable. It was a normal rebellious teenager versus parents situation coupled with the fact that my father was my coach and a coach who had to prove that he wasn't showing his daughter any favouritism over the other students. It was not easy for him and I didn't help make it easier but for a time at Kelly I think I almost came to hate him.

If one of the others had homework to do and they felt very pressured at school he would excuse them from training, if somebody else had a cold or a backache or were feeling unwell he would say, okay, you're ill, you can have the session off but if I said I was feeling ill he would say, no you're not, you are going to train. I was never allowed to have any time off. In these circumstances it would have been surprising if friction had not developed.

Another problem was the fact that Kelly was isolated out in the middle of Dartmoor. There was nowhere for us to go at all. We had swimming and we had school and nothing else. In some ways it was a little akin to being in the prison and it must have aggravated the situation with my father. Dad was still living in Plymouth while I was boarding at the school and this meant that he had to get up at 4.30 a.m. every day to drive the hour or so to the school for morning training. At the same time he and my mother were moving inexorably towards their separation and, in his squad, I was the one who was the biggest destructive influence.

In the very first days at Kelly it was new and interesting. I liked boarding school life and, as one of very few girls, I was invited for coffee with boys almost every day of the week. Marvellous confidence-building. I even found a boyfriend to help me forget Daley. But as time wore on Kelly became synonymous with tedium and boredom to me. Indeed probably more so for me and the other swimmers than for the ordinary pupils at the school. They were allowed to go into Tavistock, and have coffee, play other sports and take part in all the extra-curricular activities at the school. We had only the classroom and the pool and it was very dreary.

Initially, too, it had been expected that being at a boarding school would help our academic studies. Academic standards were much higher at Kelly and I found myself under much more pressure to work hard. Everyone had to pass an entrance examination and everyone was expected to sit at least five or six 'O' levels. Even those who were offered scholarships like myself had to pass this exam – we received no preferential treatment – and I found the change from being in the top set at Plymstock to being at a highly competitive school a quite unnerving experience.

Taken all together it led to some very unseemly scenes between me and my father. On many occasions he threw stopwatches at me in the pool – often only narrowly missing me – and I would often storm out in a rage only to have him pull me back. He would then throw me back in the pool, sometimes quite roughly, and on one occasion, accidentally, he nearly broke my nose in the process. Often we would lash out at each other and there was little love lost between us. Fortunately we were both the sort of people who flared up quickly and then forgot it equally quickly. We were like summer storms and though it must have looked like mayhem when our rows were in full swing to an outsider they were over in a flash and we would return to our work. However, I certainly did not help to make my father's life any easier.

But though I spent so much time fighting against him I couldn't stand it when other squad members criticized him. He was the coach and a coach's job is to be tough and force his pupils to go through exacting routines again and again until every muscle is screaming to stop. In the minds of all swimmers, their coaches become ogres and the swimmers curse and swear about the coach behind his back. Our squad was no different and Dad had a reputation for being somewhat of a tyrant. He was also called some very rude nicknames. Whenever he was called these names in my hearing I used to become very angry. Underneath I secretly agreed with the swimmers, my father was being very harsh and most of me went along with what they were saying. But I was still his daughter so I would rush to his defence every time. It even surprised me the extent to which I stood up for him and sometimes I felt very hypo-critical but blood is thicker than water and the Davies blood, like our hides, is pretty thick.

The press, of course, were always keen to hear news about me, and jumped on the apparent family feud with gusto. As usual, they made far more of it than it was but, this time at least, they cannot be blamed. My father and I were never very discreet about our differences of opinion. We would row no matter who was present and our fights became almost legendary in the swimming world. It was good news copy and the papers would have been very neglectful if they hadn't made the most of it. I didn't understand this then and could see no reason why they had to print such gross exaggerations.

The newspaper coverage itself added to the general tension as did the widespread speculation that Moscow might be called off because of the political situation. I was becoming bored with swimming anyway (I had been training seriously for over eight years almost non-stop) and the possibility that the reward for my training tortures might be plucked from me was almost the last straw. I was able to persevere with the agonizing and numbing training only because there was the thought of an Olympic Games and an Olympic medal at the end of it. Nothing was yet decided politically but there was much discussion of a complete boycott and it made me sick with anger and frustration. There seemed very little point in going on.

Added to all this was the fact that I had, unbeknown to me or my father, glandular fever. For weeks I had been feeling off colour and I was given the standard tests but they were negative. I didn't realize at the time that a large percentage of glandular fever cases are not detectable at first. Because of this my father thought I just had a bad cold – something swimmers suffer from for much of the time through being caught in draughts when wet – and insisted that I keep up with my training programme. So for a large part of that disastrous year I was pushing myself with the added burden of a full dose of glandular fever. It made me feel faint and weak but there was never any let up.

Glandular fever, however, was not my only medical worry. At about the same time I started to suffer from hyperventilation

A good front shot of me practising the butterfly which is a very difficult shot to take. Notice how close to the water I breathe which is very important in the butterfly
Associated Newspapers

problems. At first we thought it was a form of asthma because I was having great difficulty catching my breath but it turned out to be caused by too much oxygen in my system. The solution was simple – I just had to breathe in my own exhaled carbon dioxide to balance the system but it was an emergency I could well have done without.

Throughout the whole of this period I just was not fit for my work in the pool. The way my father used to train me was to say, right, we will swim 100 metres 10 times off 90 seconds holding 65 seconds for the swim. In ordinary terms this meant that I had to swim the 100 in 65 seconds, have 25 seconds to rest and swim again, also in 65 seconds. Such a time is not exactly slow for the 100 metres and to do it ten times in a row is tough training by anyone's standards. Usually my face would fall at such a demand but Dad would say that I was grouchy only because I couldn't do it. That would succeed in rousing me to do it just to spite him. It was a technique that suited both our characters and it worked well. During this period of illness, however, I wasn't able to jump in and show him he was wrong. No matter how hard I tried I couldn't do what he asked and, not realizing how ill I was, I began to believe that I had lost it – a belief that added fuel only to my growing desire to give up swimming. Inside I think I must have still believed I was going to Moscow because I think I would almost certainly have given it up without those games as a spur.

Everything that could have gone wrong went wrong. When I recovered from glandular fever and hyperventilation I injured my shoulder seriously. Somehow I managed to tear one of my deltoid muscles. It meant that I couldn't push and had difficulty in doing any of my exercises. Scar tissue had formed where the muscle had healed and this caused pain whenever I did anything even slightly strenuous.

We tried everything. I had cortisone treatment, physiotherapy – you name it I tried it – and nothing seemed to work. Finally we went to an osteopath and he cleared it up in a couple of weeks. It was like magic but he did say that, had I left it another two weeks before seeing him it would have fixed itself into a frozen shoulder and I would have been finished as an athlete. It was a close run thing and I will always be grateful to him.

At the time, however, I couldn't have cared less whether the shoulder healed or not. It was all pretty horrific and I was beginning to get depressed – something I had never been before. It was so bad I was close to cracking and I think I would have done so if it wasn't for Garry Richards. Garry was a very young go-ahead gym owner who ran a small club in Tavistock. Early in the year Garry had been approached by my father because he felt that we should use a proper gym. Garry had agreed readily and I could use the gym whenever I wanted. After my 'O' levels I took a little time off from school and would spend my training time in Garry's gym though not so much to train as to cry on Garry's shoulder. He was wonderful. He would raise my spirits and keep me going and be a friend – which was, of course, just what I needed. Garry would buy me films and take me out on the moors on photography trips. The thought that, at last, I had someone who understood helped to keep me going. Often Garry would try to act as an intermediary between me and my father but Dad's reaction was usually to say, 'Don't be so stupid, she is just being childish' and completely dismiss all my heart-pourings to which Garry had been kind and patient enough to listen. After a while he realized it was a waste of time trying to plead my case so he gave up and just concerned himself with being an available shoulder and friend.

My father has since apologized for some of the things he did. He knows that the attitude he adopted was too rigid but he was a self-taught coach and everything he was doing then was an experiment. I was his guinea pig as well as being the best female swimmer in Britain. Dad was learning all the time without the experience of having another comparable swimmer in my class. I am certain now that whenever he picked on me it was with the very best intentions but he just did not understand. He had not the faintest idea of what goes on in the mind of an adolescent girl and whenever he came up against something he didn't understand he took it as rebellion and reacted in the only way he knew. Today he is much wiser and much more experienced. The swimmers he has under his care now are all benefiting from the mistakes he made with me and they are lucky to have such a good coach – in my opinion the very best in Britain.

It has to be admitted, too, that it rarely works for any athlete to have a parent as a coach. The coach–athlete relationship must, by definition, be based on authority. The coach is the boss and the athlete must obey. But most teenagers at some stage rebel against their parents and I had to rebel against my coach as well. The fact that we survived together at all only really shows just how deep the bond is between us. Despite all our ups and downs we always maintained a very special relationship and I love him as much for his well-intentioned failures as for his successes.

Another reason the year was a bit of a damp squib was that there were very few competitions. There were some home internationals but nothing of any consequence and I didn't even have the adrenalin flow and excitement of competition as a reviver for my flagging enthusiasm. Towards the end of 1979 I was so bored that my father was desperately trying to find some way of injecting some enthusiasm again to have a chance of the Olympic medal we both wanted so much.

To do my father justice I have to say that he wasn't totally blind to what was going on and maybe some of the things Garry said to him had an effect because, towards the end of 1979, he arranged a trip to Texas for training. Knowing how much good the visit to Toronto had done two years before, he hoped that a new environment and new people were among the things I needed to lift me out of myself. Earlier in the year there had been a problem about arranging such a trip because we had lost our Rollei sponsorship and there was no one to meet the bills. Now he had been successful in arranging for Wimpey Construction to put up some money and Texas was chosen.

I was very excited at the prospect of training overseas again. The year had been much harder on me than the others in the squad, if only because they could go home in holidays and half-terms and train with others, whereas I had to stay and train alone in the Kelly pool with just my father for company. Just the thought of swimming in a different pool was enough to raise my spirits.

Perhaps one of the reasons I felt so low during most of 1979 was due to the fact that I had, stupidly perhaps, given up school immediately after sitting my 'O' levels. I didn't think it was worthwhile

Giving a helping hand to another squad member, American Annabel
Cripps, before a warm-up in December 1979
Associated Newspapers

starting an 'A' level course so I just used to sit around at Kelly between training sessions. It was during this time that I started becoming ill and it was when I began to cry on Garry's shoulder. Now, of course, I could kick myself for giving up my schoolwork. I could have at least started a course and, if necessary, continued it later at evening classes. Instead I just sat there feeling sorry for myself and making everybody else's life hell. I looked forward to the Texas trip very much as I imagine a prisoner sees the day of his release.

The trip was to the University of Austin where an American coach called Paul Bergen trained one of the top American swimmers, Tracey Caulkins. I didn't enjoy the visit.

From the outset I didn't get on with Bergen and I didn't like the atmosphere of training in a university. It was a bit like training in a factory. Added to that I found the Americans themselves annoyingly over-the-top. It was as though they had made a national game out of being polite. In England people are polite, and often quite formal, but in the States they always behave as though they have known you for several years, even if you have only just met.

So even the eagerly anticipated trip to Texas was a failure in that black year. My parents' marriage was breaking up and I was close to cracking and every day was grey. I couldn't wait for New Year and the thought of starting afresh. It would be 1980, the year that I had worked towards ever since I had made the decision to become a competitive swimmer. Ten years of training would be tested in a matter of minutes in a swimming pool and I was determined, despite the family wrangles and the difficulties of growing up, not to let either my family or myself down. I was not ready for it and my times were nowhere near good enough but I just hoped that, as 1979 had been the blackest year of my life, so 1980 might be the best.

CHAPTER SEVEN

Moment of Truth

Two developments, neither of them much in themselves, happened at the beginning of 1980 and, between them, they changed my life. The first was that I passed my driving test. Mobility gives a wonderful feeling of freedom and just being able to drive the car on my own from Plymouth to Kelly was a tonic. It was a sign of independence. All I needed now was something to occupy my free moments and it would be plain sailing towards recovery and better times. That something came in the form of Sam . . . a Red Setter. I have always, and still have, a passion for dogs and I sorely missed not having one while I was at Kelly. Most of my earliest childhood memories included dogs, and, at the beginning of this, my most testing year, I pleaded for one again. My mother was against the idea. She was beginning to enjoy having more freedom now that my brothers were older and was reluctant to tie herself to looking after a dog again. But my father realized that I needed something to take my mind off my troubles and so he bought me Sam; he was a lifesaver. With Sam and the car I had freedom. I used to take him out on the moors and spend hours just walking and playing with him. I would always take a camera with me and between that and Sam there was always enough to keep me occupied and active.

As I have already said I should have been taking at least one 'A' level. I had always wanted to sit three so that I could go to University, study English and take up a career in journalism. I didn't have the two years available that would have been necessary to complete a full 'A' level course but I could have crammed the study for one subject into one year and at least started. But I didn't, I regret it now but I was pig-headed then and so I allowed the opportunity to slip away. Sam was all I wanted to keep me happy – he became my life when I was not actually in the pool.

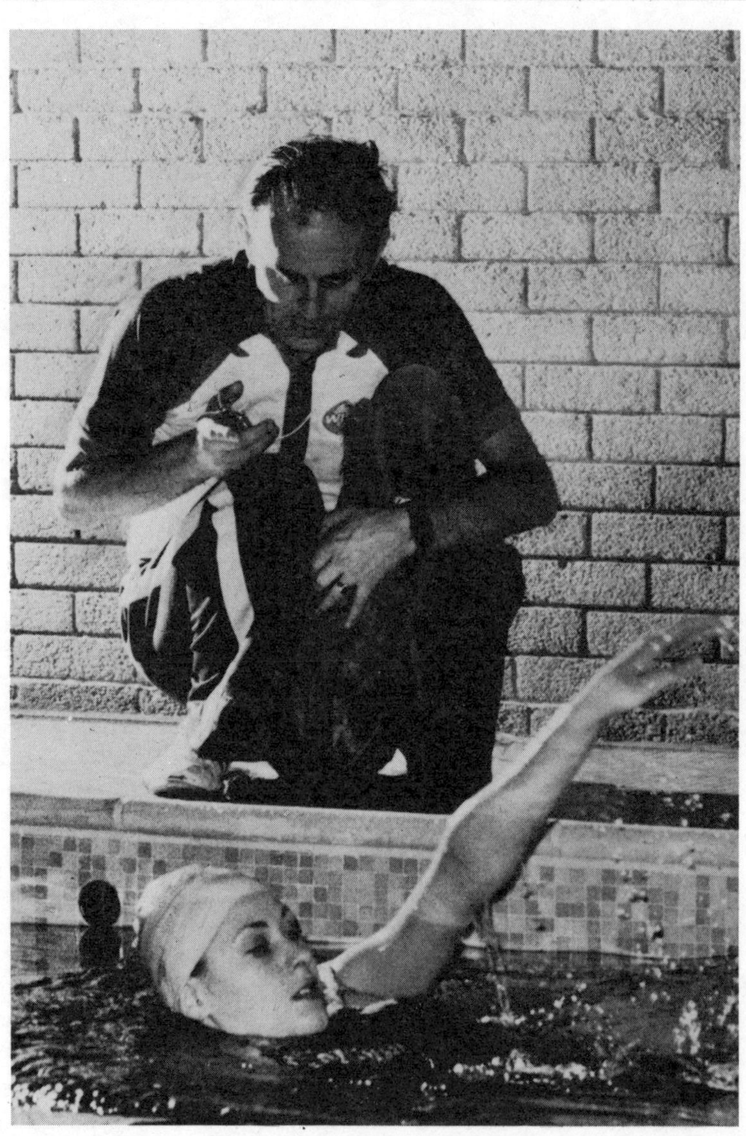

Dad and Sam watch me train in the pool at Kelly College in March 1980
Associated Newspapers

Now that I felt happier within myself my swimming started to pick up automatically. At a meeting at Barnet Copthall quite early in the year I did particularly well. I don't think this competition is held any more but it used to be sponsored by an electrical company and the prizes were all electrical appliances. It was of quite a high standard – most of Britain's best swimmers would take part – and it was a good way of building up one's confidence for the competition. For me it was also a bonanza. I won three black and white portable television sets, three cassette recorders and several clock radio/calculators. They were easily the most useful things I had ever won. My brothers, naturally, wanted most of them but I gave some to my grandfather who was in hospital and I was delighted to be able to dispense this largesse. The competition was not of international level but it was a promising beginning and, from that competition on, I started to tackle my work with greater relish.

In April the Short Course Championships came around again and I was returning to my old form again. I always enjoyed the Short Course because it was held in the smaller buildings that housed the smaller pools. Somehow there was always better atmosphere in these more enclosed places. The spectators would be sitting that much nearer to the swimmers. There was always a greater sense of comradeship and a much jollier inter-club rivalry. The Short Course had always been my favourite event for the lighter side of competing, and, now that 1979 was over, I thoroughly enjoyed becoming involved in the spirit of swimming again. The pressure was never very great at the Short Course. Swimmers used it as a way of building-up and the atmosphere was one of people swimming for fun. It was just what I needed. It reminded me that swimming was more than stop watches and repetitive routines and I started to look ahead to the Olympics, only three months away, with enthusiasm again. The incentive had returned and I knew I could succeed. Winning that long-sought-after medal returned as the raison d'être of my life.

I didn't walk away with that Short Course as on previous occasions but the writing was on the wall again and I knew inside that hitting my peak was only a short time away.

In fact, it came quicker than I had dared hope. At an invitational meet between Britain and Sweden at Blackpool only a matter of weeks later I broke the Commonwealth record for the 200 individual medley again. It surprised everyone; not least me. Although I was climbing back I was still off form and breaking that record was an unexpected bonus. Of all the records I had broken I suppose that one was the easiest to improve on: but I lowered it by about two tenths of a second only. For some strange reason the 200 medley record was the one I never brought down as much as perhaps I could have done. For about two years I had been clocking 2 minutes 16 seconds frequently in training and the record stood at 2 minutes 17 seconds so I should really have been able to shatter it with the extra impetus of a race on my side. Because I did not reduce the time sufficiently the record is no longer mine – it was squeezed away from me by two tenths of a second at the Brisbane Commonwealth Games – and I wish only that I could have my time over again to make that record secure. I am sure that with just a little more application I could have made it virtually unattainable; at least for swimmers from non-steroid countries!

Still I was happy enough with my time and my progress and happier still that I had a new boyfriend. He was a Swedish swimmer, and before long quite a serious relationship was developing. I met him at a party after the meeting ended and I liked him immediately. He felt the same and, as we were staying in Blackpool, we decided to go for a long walk along the promenade. While we were gone, the Swedish and British teams were taken home and when we returned the party was dead. This meant that we had to walk from one end of Blackpool to the other and it was 3 a.m. by the time I arrived back at my hotel. I knew I would be in trouble but I was quite unprepared for the sight that greeted me on the hotel steps.

Waiting outside in the cold were the chaperone, the head coach and the manager. I was slightly anxious because I knew that some had been thrown out of the team for less. I felt like a naughty schoolgirl as I walked past them but I was $17\frac{1}{2}$ and I was annoyed that they were treating me like a child. As I passed, the manager grunted, 'I'll speak to you in the morning', and I thought I was in very serious trouble but nothing more was said about it . . . probably, I think, because they didn't want to cause a rumpus so close to the Olympics. It almost certainly had nothing to do with any softening of their attitudes – swimming officials never do that.

After Blackpool I went back to Kelly for a very long spell of training – but this time without the old difficulties. I felt fit again and the medal I so badly wanted was tantalisingly near. I threw myself into the work and I concentrated on nothing other than becoming faster and keener than ever before. There were few meets of any significance to break the training routine and I had entered nothing until the National Championships in late May. These were to be followed by National Time Trials immediately afterwards, (one example of the rather peculiar thinking that went on in the backrooms of the ASA). I was not too concerned with these as I had met the qualifying times early in the year but the ASA, in its wisdom, never picks its team early. It exercises slightly more pressure on swimmers than the AAA does on its athletes but if you have made the qualifying times, and they are usually quite stiff for Olympic Games, then you can be reasonably certain that you will be chosen. I had these times under my belt and no one else was even near them so I knew that, unless the ASA disapproved of me personally, there was no way they could leave me out of the team. The only obstacle that could prevent me from going to Moscow was Afghanistan.

Everyone, in all sports, was on tenterhooks. We knew it was a political problem and we were anxiously waiting for the Government to decide, 'No, you cannot go' or 'We don't think you ought to go'. I respected Mrs Thatcher's decision. Although she said that she would prefer us not to compete, she left it to each individual's conscience. She tried to find a compromise between all viewpoints. Those who had strong political feelings could adopt a position of principle and those who wanted to go were able to without feeling that they were letting anyone down. Obviously 95 per cent of the athletes wanted to go. They had trained too long and too hard to let the chance of going to the Olympics slip away because of international politics but, in some sports anyway, the decision of whether or not to go was taken away from the individual and taken over by the national organisation of the sport. I found this absurd. The Government's view had been simple and clear cut – individuals who wanted to make a point could stay at home. But some of the

Federations, Hockey and Equestrian to name two, decided to make their own political stand and ban their athletes from going even if they so wished. By this action they were bringing politics right into the heart of sport and destroying its very essence. There is never a problem when matters of this nature are left to the individual conscience but when Federations start to interfere they set up a series of chain reactions that lead to wars within their own sports and wars between the Federations. It was crazy.

In my opinion, the withdrawal of the United States was futile as it showed the Russian people only that it was not a free country after all. To react as violently as the Americans was, in my view, the very worst thing that they could have done. I know that many of the swimmers wanted to go – indeed it was a disaster for them that they could not. Swimming is similar to gymnastics in that it is rare for an athlete to compete in two Olympics; and almost unknown for someone to win medals at both. So for the American swimmers this was their only chance to carry home spoils from the top competition in the world and they were being denied that opportunity by a Government that trampled on the basic tenets of its own constitutional philosophy. Many of their swimmers were angry and I can hardly blame them.

Most British athletes had achieved results in their sports by hard work and personal sacrifice, both physical and financial. The Government never stepped in, as in the Soviet Union, to say 'you show promise, we'll train you up for nothing', it just left us to cope on our own and yet they were now trying to imply that we owed them loyalty – at the same time that Britain was continuing to trade with the Soviet Union.

I think also that our action of going to Moscow but refusing to take part in the opening ceremony or use the British flag was very effective. It caused the ordinary Russian to ask questions which could not be so easily explained away as the absence of the Americans. Obviously I felt sad when the Olympic flag went up in place of the Union Jack at my own medal ceremony. In my opinion, there is never a good reason for boycotting the Olympics. However, I am too realistic to think that we will ever have a non-political games.

Before the Games the ASA kept swimmers waiting for a decision until the very last moment. The Association was the last of the Federations to make up its mind and it was a trying time for us. We watched in horror as the Hockey Federation and then the Equestrian plumped for staying at home and we were afraid that the ASA, for which few of us had much respect, would opt to stay at home.

Fortunately, they finally came down on the side of sanity and decided to go but not before discussing a variety of alternatives, one of which was competing in the American Nationals instead of Moscow. The Americans had decided to hold their own championships immediately after the Moscow Games and to post up the Olympic times before the start of each race. The idea was that if their swimmers beat the Olympic time they could claim to be the real Olympic champions. It was designed by their own Federation as a way to motivate their swimmers but it didn't work. They were all so despondent at not being at a proper Olympics that the meeting flopped. Some of them swam very well, of course, because they had trained properly and were at peak fitness but some of them told me later that the atmosphere was heavy with gloom and bitterness. I feel sorry for them, especially Tracey Caulkins who I came to know quite well. Tracey is a great swimmer but now she will never have an Olympic medal. It is true she did win five golds at a World Championships but any swimmer will tell you that the World Championships don't bear any comparison to the Olympics and I am quite sure Tracey would have quite gladly swapped all of those five medals for just one Olympic Championship.

In England the press were insatiable for news, and no matter where I went hordes of them would crowd round to ask me what I thought of Margaret Thatcher. I had views, of course, but at the time I didn't want to make any public statement and I became very annoyed by this non-stop harassment. After a time I took to giving a short, stock answer: I would say, quickly, 'She's a politician and she had to say what she did – I am a swimmer and I have to go.' It summed up my view without being too controversial but it still did not satisfy them and they continued to pester me right up until the aeroplane took off.

Once the ASA had made the decision to go the swimming preparation fell into an uncannily familiar routine. There was the usual three-week training camp at Crystal Palace with the hostel providing the same foods that I couldn't eat (reminiscent of school dinners of red meat and spotted dick) and the same voice, characteristic of a holiday camp, using the intercom every few minutes from 8 a.m. onwards with a voice as cloying as Golden Syrup saying: 'Good morning, it's 5 (or 10 or 15, etc.) minutes past 8, breakfast will be served in . . .'. I think I came to loathe that woman's voice especially as she was calling us to a communal meal that, for me anyway, was completely inedible. The only way I could keep going was to supplement my diet with sweets and biscuits (strictly forbidden!) but I still lost half-a-stone: for me about par for the Crystal Palace course.

In the training pool the coaching was not to my liking either. I was back with the national coaches (my father had to stay out of the way), and they didn't take any notice of individual requirements. In swimming terms, I had grown up and I no longer had to train as much as before. This was not out of laziness, it is just that, as you grow older in swimming the quantity of training should fall off and the quality of the swimming should improve. The coaches were still trying to put quantity with quality and I was still required to put in many miles. I knew it was wrong for me but I was unable to convince anyone else. When we arrived in Moscow I took matters into my own hands and coached myself. I was painfully aware that the length-after-length style of coaching was getting me nowhere. It was a rebellion again on my part but I was positive I knew what was best for me and was eventually proved right with a British and Commonwealth record. I was not 'flavour of the month' with the management, however. I was far, far too headstrong and independent for their liking.

I had started to antagonize the ASA even earlier when we were still at Crystal Palace. For reasons that I have never understood the Association had brought along medical testing equipment to test all the top swimmers. They had decided to find out whether we were fit or not . . . one week before we were due to leave to take part in a major event! I could not believe that they were serious. There was no way I was going to let them test me. I knew in myself whether I was ready or not and if I wasn't fit in the opinion of their machines I simply did not want to know. It would not have done my morale

With Duncan Goodhew at Heathrow Airport before leaving for
Moscow in July 1980. Duncan has always thought I had long legs!
London Express News

or confidence much good if a machine pronounced that I was not ready. I had to go and compete in any event and I was damned if I was going to put up with a final thumbs up or thumbs down from a robot. I was the only one who adopted this attitude but I adopted it because I believed the ASA was implementing something that was pointless and possibly harmful to the athlete. No one supported my stand, however, and I was beginning to make some enemies in the backrooms of the sport: faceless enemies who were able to wield their moment of power later.

I would not have objected in the slightest if they had produced their testing machines six months before the Games. Then, if there was something wrong it could have been cured with time to spare. But to come along one week before leaving was too much.

Compared with the fanfares that heralded our departure for the Montreal Olympics four years earlier, the departure for Moscow was rather like sneaking out of the back door.

There were still many well wishers and the press were present in force but it was all a much more low key affair. All the companies who had been sponsoring the Games in January had pulled out because of the Afghanistan situation. The towelling manufacturers wouldn't supply us with towels and many of the other goods that we had been supplied with for Montreal were simply not made available. Even the general budget was low because a large part of funds that had been promised to the Olympic Association did not materialize. Instead of boarding the aeroplane laden down with suitcases of free equipment, we had little more than we could fit into our pockets. It was disheartening that so many people were obviously so violently opposed to our attending these Games and we all felt rather dejected when we mounted the aircraft steps. It didn't last very long because we were all keyed up to go and take part in an event for which we had been preparing for years; and that led to some high spirits. Anyway we were determined to show everyone at home, whether they approved or not, that it was worth our while going.

I could hardly contain my excitement. Just being on an aeroplane was enough to set my heart racing. I loved flying and I was very keen to take my pilot's licence so I asked if I could go up and visit the captain on the flight deck. Not only did he agree but he also let me stay there during the approach to Moscow airport. It was strictly illegal but they knew I was interested in learning to fly and so they let me witness a landing at first-hand. In fact, the captain said, I could be a help to them. He wanted me to listen to the radio and see if I could help them fathom out just what the Russian air traffic controllers were saying. I couldn't of course. The mixture of Russian and bad English that was coming over the airwaves was worse than double dutch and there was no way that any of us could understand a word. When we had landed I asked the pilot how on earth had he known where to land? Apparently he had had to land like that on a previous occasion when he hadn't been able to understand air traffic control very well either.

From that cockpit I gained my first impression of the Soviet Union. The airport looked busy and crowded with aeroplanes but the captain pointed out to me that most of the aeroplanes were fakes. Some had no engines and some no interiors but they had been scattered about to give the foreign visitors an example of the Soviet Union's power and prosperity. It was pitiful really because on closer inspection it was obvious that these so-called aircraft were just derelict: they hadn't even bothered to paint them. To a Russian it obviously looked like a busy airport going about its business but to a Westener it looked like a scrapyard. Of course, this helped our pilot as he used these dummy planes to guide his approach.

It was an early insight for me into what I should expect in the Soviet Union and I was not disappointed.

We were more or less the first people to arrive in the Olympic village itself. There were a few other foreign teams around, probably swimmers because of the early start, but there wasn't a Russian in sight. We were guests in their country but we were not allowed to mix freely with the locals; or perhaps vice versa and the Russian team was kept well away from the village in a big hotel until the very last moment. Normally, as the overseas teams arrive there is plenty of fun and mixing socially in the village but, this time, it was obvious that the Russians wanted to keep their team as far away as possible from Westerners for as long as possible. We didn't even see any locals because we had been rushed straight to the village. It was more like being in a ghetto than an international meeting of athletes.

All was drab and the same. The standard of the building was atrocious and there was no trace of any individuality. Everything was a uniform, plain-faced, flat – rather like the worst type of 1960s' council flats in Britain – and it was incredibly depressing. We knew that after the Games people would be living in them and thinking themselves lucky for the privilege. These were apartments for numbers not individuals and I was shocked – especially as they were being held up as examples of the enormous advantages of their political system. They would not have allowed foreign athletes to stay in them unless they were proud of them.

They did make an effort to set up a community-cum-recreation area in the village but they staged only ballets and operas, which were not widely popular and they supplied an ancient music centre with two records – one by Elton John and one by Cliff Richard (because both Elton and Cliff had toured the Soviet Union) – and an ice cream shop, which was hard to find but worth it if you did because the ice cream was delicious. The two records, of course, were played to death and the ballet and opera companies were more often than not playing to an empty house. Apart from the cafeteria, however, this was the only entertainment and it was not surprising that people were bored. It wasn't as if we could leave the village and go somewhere else because there was only the village. It was miles from anywhere and quite some distance from the city itself: quite obviously we were intended to be kept as isolated as possible. They had built a 25-metre pool and an athletics track in the village so that athletes could train without going to the actual venues but, even so, people spent much time twiddling their thumbs.

It was a huge village with 24 men's blocks and 12 women's blocks (the men's were painted blue and the women's pink just in case you forgot where you were!) and the only way of travelling around was to use the internal bus service that had been provided. The buses would drive around inside the perimeter fence around which stony-faced, armed guards were posted every ten yards or so. For some light relief we used to take the bus to some point along the perimeter and then get out to speak to the guards. None of them could speak English but we used to smile and wink at them and if they didn't smile or wink back we would throw paper cups at them. If they were more responsive, one of us would go up and stick a badge in their pockets. They all wanted these badges but they would have been severely punished if they had been seen asking for them so we just gave badges to the more friendly ones.

There were not many friendly ones, however. Indeed most were very wary and scared and they tried their hardest to ignore us when we tossed things at them. The extent to which the Russians were nervous about this was almost unbelievable. One day, not long after our arrival, I watched for three hours as a non-stop procession of coaches transported all the children out of the city. It was early in the morning when this sad convoy motored past the village and I was one of only a few people to see it. It was disturbing to say the least. It was obvious to me that they were taking all the children away so that they would be in no danger of coming into contact with any of us. The Russian authorities knew that the visiting teams in Moscow planned to make protests by not using their national flags and by boycotting the opening ceremony and they did not want their children to ask embarrassing questions about why this was happening. To stop it they sent them to stay in the country where they would watch only doctored television reports of the Games. We were told that the children were ferried off to camps every year but it seems too much of a coincidence to me that it happened just a week before the Olympics and I cannot believe that it was normal to ship them out like that.

Later I saw some pictures that these Russian kids had painted and one of them was of me. I don't know why I was chosen and whether or not I had a little fan in the Soviet Union but I was very touched by it. The Russians hung these paintings in an exhibition and they were filmed by British television. I still have a video of it and will always wonder who painted it.

But whoever painted it was not present at the Games and it was quite disconcerting. There is something very eerie about being in a city with no kids. There were plenty of parks and playgrounds but no kids in them and it made Moscow seem half-dead. I was not at all sad when I left.

It was during this last week before the competition started that I made my decision to become my own coach. The technique of length after length that the coaches were using was not working with me and I decided to go it alone. My father was in Moscow but he wasn't there to advise me when I was in the pool so I took the law into my own hands and started a training schedule I devised myself. Instead of doing great yardage I started to concentrate on technique and I did just enough yardage to keep me sharp. I knew I had the strength and I knew that I didn't need the extra strength build-up that came with distance. What I needed was speed and that came from refining the technique. I worked on this alone, away from the official coaches and, slowly, I reached a point where my mental and physical edge was as match sharp as it had ever been. I was ready.

The question of politics reared its head again for the opening ceremony and lots were drawn to find six or ten people who would march around behind an Olympic flag. I watched that sad opening on television because I had caught a virus and had to stay inside but the majority of the swimming team were swimming during the ceremony – training.

It was as though we were there to compete and nothing else. There was nothing friendly about these Games – there was no comparison with the Edmonton Commonwealth Games – we were there just to do our job and then leave. Indeed when all the swimmers had competed we were on an aeroplane on our way home just as soon as we finished swimming. There was no lingering and certainly no closing ceremony, at least as far as we were concerned.

My first competitive event was the 400 freestyle. It wasn't an event in which I stood to win a medal – though I did just miss qualifying for the final – but it did give me an opportunity to see how the competitions were organized, such as the routine for marching out. It was quite a good day for the Brits because it was the day Duncan Goodhew won his 100 breaststroke. It gave the whole of our camp a bit of a boost and made me more than ever determined to show that I could win a medal too.

I don't want to detract from Duncan's success in any way, but it was one of the events which was devastated by the absence of the Americans, West Germans and Canadians. The world record holder was a West German and the Americans had four competitors who had swum faster than Duncan at their National Championships and Duncan had been well beaten by a Canadian called Graham Smith two years earlier at Edmonton so, though his win lifted our morale, we knew that other races would not be similarly affected. We kept our feet on the ground and we were a very professional team – perhaps the most professional I had been part of. Along with the rest I rejoiced that Duncan had his medal to take home but I knew my event was as daunting as ever as it was not affected at all by the absence of the big teams; the East German women were present.

Everyone in our team did all that could have been asked of them and many came up with personal best times. We were all determined and were reaching the finals in events that the press had given us no chance of surviving the heats. Being with those swimmers was stimulating and encouraging. We supported each other and we considered ourselves a team rather than a group of individuals. The fantastic spirit went a long way towards compensating us for the misery of the Games themselves and I am grateful to all of them for giving me such good memories besides winning a medal in Moscow.

Two days after Duncan's gold I had the heats of the 400 medley in the morning. Under the 'before Games' seeding system which was used I was the third fastest qualifier. As there were three heats of eight people it meant that the fastest qualifier swam in the centre lane in the third heat, the second fastest the centre lane in the second heat with me in the centre lane in the very first heat. This meant that I had to set the time because swimming is not like athletics where the first two in each heat and the two fastest losers make the final. In swimming, everything is judged by time and I could win my heat and still not make the final if eight others in the following heats bettered my time.

So my task was to produce a time that would make the final but not sap all of my strength. I had a Russian girl next to me who I knew quite well and, with her as a pacemaker, I produced a time of 4 minutes 52 seconds which put me in lane seven in the final as fifth fastest qualifier. I wasn't too disappointed with that but I would have been happier if I had qualified closer to the centre. My personal best time at that stage was 4 minutes 47 seconds and so 5 seconds slower over 400 metres in a heat was not bad. I would have had a better chance of seeing what was going on around me if I had been in the centre lanes but I knew I still had a chance in lane seven – after all it was 400 metres, it wasn't as though it was a sprint.

The next stage was a light lunch – a very light lunch because the adrenalin was gnawing away at my stomach – and a shave down. Most swimmers do this before a race and it requires shaving down the whole of the body that comes into contact with the water. It is not that it makes you any faster – or, if it does it is quite insignificant, perhaps thousandths of a second – it just makes you feel as if you are going faster. After a shave down the whole body tingles as soon as it hits the water and you can feel yourself sliding through it. It is a marvellous feeling and it gives a very definite psychological boost. Even Duncan Goodhew, who doesn't have any body hair at all naturally, shaves down his body to give himself this terribly important lift before a race. It is simply a case of, 'if you feel good you will do well' and we all wanted to give ourselves whatever little help there was on offer.

At 4.45 p.m. I caught the bus back to the Olympic pool with my stomach tied in a knot with nerves. I don't think I had ever been quite as nervous before any other race of my career and my body was producing adrenalin so fast it was making me feel sick. However, once in the pool for a warm-up everything seemed to settle and my nerves, though not vanishing altogether, gave way to a steely resolve that I wasn't going to allow this one to slip away.

Just before the final itself we were gathered together in one room, divided into lanes and marched up the side of the pool. At 17 I was the second oldest of the eight finalists, the East German girl who had won the Montreal Olympics, Ulrika Taulber, was the oldest, and I was the only swimmer from a non-Communist country. It was very encouraging because it meant that all of the other teams and their supporters at the pool, the French and the Australians in particular, were shouting for me. It was as though I represented the whole of the West and it made me feel very proud. I knew too that with the volume of support they were giving me I would be able to produce my very best.

Of course, at the same time I felt under extreme pressure and just a little dwarfed surrounded by three East Germans, two Poles, a Russian and a Czech. The East German world record holder had the centre lane advantage and I was next to Ulrika Taulber who was the one I had to beat. Ulrika had been an Olympic gold medallist and a world record holder (she had lost it to another East German only recently) and to be sure of a medal I had to beat her so I was glad she was in the lane next to mine where I could keep an eye on her.

I was a bit worried by some of the other girls because I knew little about them but I did know that Ulrika was fast and, if I was faster, there would probably be a medal in it.

When I climbed onto the block just before the start I looked up into the crowd and saw my father who gave me a quick sign of encouragement and then, almost before I knew it, it was take your marks and off. The first stroke was butterfly and at the changeover into backstroke after two lengths I was in fourth place, about where I would have expected. Backstroke was my second strongest and I turned third after that leg – up one place. Ulrika Taulber, who was on my inside, was just behind me and I was worried that on the breaststroke leg, my weakest, she would flash past and I would have much to make up in the two lengths of freestyle to the finish.

As I turned from the backstroke into the breaststroke leg I remember thinking to myself: 'What the hell am I doing here? Here I am hurting like crazy and for what, I must be an idiot.' It was a strange thing to think at that time as I had never thought like that before. It lasted only a second and I was able to thrust it from my mind and get on with the job in hand but I will always remember thinking it and I will always wonder why it bubbled up just at that particular time.

At the end of the breaststroke I was exhausted. I had put every ounce of effort I possessed into it and, to my delight, had ended it still in third place. At the point of turning I caught sight of the Polish girl in second place on the far side of the pool. She had already turned, perhaps a second and a half in front, as I began what I knew was my strongest leg. My medal hopes were very high.

At the end of the race I was a second and a half ahead of that

Polish girl – I had taken three seconds off her in the freestyle and I was second: the silver medallist. When I made that final touch and turned round to see the clock the relief was incredible. As far as I was concerned the Olympics were over and finished. Of course they were not as I still had to swim in the relays but the pressure was now off and I could enjoy my moment of triumph. And I very much wanted to enjoy that moment. It was the culmination of ten years' hard work and, coming on top of the deep depression of the year before, the most rewarding and satisfying moment of my life. What I had achieved, measured up to every hope and expectation. The East German girl who beat me had done so by a full nine seconds – she had even taken four seconds off the world record – but she really had a man's body and there was no way anyone could beat 'her'. She was massive with no breasts and a voice that was more baritone than soprano. I hadn't been beaten by a swimmer. I had been beaten by a drug and I wasn't at all disappointed. I had still shaved a second off my own Commonwealth record and I had my silver medal: the medal at which I had been aiming. Even two years earlier, whenever my father was asked what we were training for he would say the Olympic silver medal. He knew I could never beat the East German tank – no one could – and I was always coached to be the best of the rest. In fact it was even better than that from a satisfaction viewpoint because all the girls I had beaten in the race had, at some stage or other, been on steroids and I had beaten them without this artificial aid. It was the greatest thrill of my life and I felt giddy and deliriously happy as I climbed out of the pool; especially as I knew that, even if the Americans and all the other teams had been there, I would still have finished a medallist.

At the US Championships that followed, Tracey Caulkins beat my time slightly and it is possible that, had she raced, she may have beaten me. But it is almost certain that she would not have swum in the medley. Her main event, the 100 metres breaststroke, was in the same session and she would have opted for that and not entered the medley. This means that I hold my Olympic silver with a completely clear conscience; there is no one walking around feeling aggrieved that Sharron Davies has a medal that was rightfully theirs. I won it on merit and my pride in that achievement is undiluted.

A very special moment. Relieved and jubilant after winning the silver medal in the 400 metres individual medley at the Moscow Olympics
London Express News

Tracey had recently been the world record holder in the 100 breaststroke and to win a gold, she would have concentrated on that event. She realized that she stood no chance against the East German in the medley so, had the Americans been in Moscow, it is certain Tracey would not have been competing against me and my honour was satisfied.

I say now that I couldn't have been happier with the result but, in fact, that isn't quite true. The East German winner could have, and I believe, should have, been disqualified. The rules of breaststroke swimming require the swimmer to keep the head above the water; it is forbidden for the water to immerse the whole body. She did just that. She had been disqualified on a previous occasion because of it and she was to be disqualified again at the next World Championships. But those Championships were held in the West and these Olympics were held in the Soviet Union. She had broken the rules and she should have been censured for it but the Russians turned a blind eye. Of course, I realize that even if she had had her legs tied together she could still have beaten me but it is an example of the injustices existing in the sport. It is still true, however, that had the Games been held in any country outside Eastern Europe, I would have been the Gold Medallist.

Indeed the Russians were very flexible in their interpretation of the rules in Moscow. In one of the relay races their team didn't turn up until ten minutes after the rest of the teams had lined up at the start. In any other country they would have been disqualified immediately but, because it was the Soviet Union, no action was taken. Everyone else was standing around in their costumes waiting to start and getting cold and the Russians just sauntered out when they were ready. It was quite inexcusable but the Russians made a mockery of the rules and did whatever they liked to suit themselves. If the Americans had been present, there would have been numerous protests but the Russians were able to conduct these truncated Games as they wished and were virtually unchallenged. Our own officials were completely impotent against them.

After the blood test and the drug test – rather ironical considering I was standing beside the East German girl – came one of the most emotional moments of my life: standing on the rostrum and receiv-

My most important medal ceremony. Right: A. Czopek who took the bronze and centre: Petra Schneider who won the gold

Allsport

ing my medal. I was saddened when the Olympic flag was hoisted up instead of the Union Jack – there is very little that inspires the patriot in me as much as the sight of that flag – but, at the same time I was pleased that it was a sign of Britain's disapproval of the Soviet intervention in Afghanistan and in my view a much more effective protest than the total boycott by the others. I felt my medal was also, in a way, a victory against the Soviets which made me even prouder still.

From the victory rostrum I looked up into the vast crowd which surrounded me and saw my father. He was grinning from ear to ear and I couldn't wait to be with him and to share this moment with him. However, it was longer than I expected. The problem was that one of the dope tests they do after an event is a urine test.

Before a race all the adrenalin racing around makes you want to rush to the lavatory all the time but after a race it is almost impossible to go. It is also difficult as someone is always watching to make sure you don't cheat which is very degrading and very inhibiting! It was hours before I had enough for the required specimen but, when I had managed it, I found my father outside waiting for me. He had waited three hours to see me and had missed his last bus back to his hotel. That first moment of meeting after the medal, however, was very special to both of us. We embraced with very few words and I think there were tears in my eyes as we hugged each other for joy. All the rows and scenes were forgotten as we revelled in our joint success. We had achieved it together and now was the time for celebration. Unfortunately the celebration turned out to be a couple of sore feet for Dad. He had to walk all the way back to his hotel – a distance of about four or five miles – but if he was as happy as I was he would have made very light work of it. He probably wouldn't have been able to sleep anyway: I know I couldn't. All that night I lay awake going over and over the race in my mind. I should really have tried harder to sleep as I had a relay the next day but I couldn't and the result was that I wasn't anywhere near my best in the relay itself. I was still too tired and too full of my medal to concentrate totally and we could do no better than fourth. It was a pity because if three of the four of us had swum at our personal best times we probably would have taken home another medal.

I had some spare time after my events were finished to sightsee around Moscow and, quite frankly, I was appalled by what I saw. I didn't visit too many of the standard sights but I saw the average conditions Russians had to put up with every day and it made me feel more than a little sad.

I found the drabness and dreariness of the city a little depressing. There was nothing in the shops that anyone would want to buy and what there was was far too expensive for the average Russian worker to buy. The black market was rife and one was given up to ten times the official exchange rate for foreign currency. Those who were caught, of course, were severely punished but the only way they could buy the luxury western goods that were on sale was with foreign currency and they would do almost anything for it.

The cleanest place that I found was the Moscow underground which is built of marble with chandeliers and statues on every station. It is very impressive and so are the trains but it is nearly impossible to travel on them because of the smell. Muscovites might have a good underground system but they do not use deodorant. I remember travelling on a packed train in the rush hour on my way to visit my father in his hotel and having to hold my nose to stop myself passing out.

But there was more than just the condition of the Russian people on my mind. I also began to worry about our swimmers: they were becoming restless. All their events were over, they had time on their hands, the pressure was off and they wanted to have a good time. But there was nothing to do except make mischief. There were two and a half days to fill after all the swimming events were over – we had to wait for a few of the athletes who were sharing our aeroplane to finish – and the only occupation our people could find to entertain them was food fights. It wasn't because we were terribly crazy or anything like that. It was just that everyone had trained for up to ten years for this competition, we had been together over a month and a half during the final preparation and now it was all over, there was a natural desire to release some tension. The food fights were just one of those silly things.

If they could have gone into the city and been invited to parties as they had in Montreal there would have been no trouble at all but they were exiled in the village with nothing but two well-worn Elton John and Cliff Richard records. It is true the Russians did try to stage an apology for a disco every night but it was over with the lights out by 11.30 p.m.

Of course, it was asking for trouble. Those who had just finished competing in a major event were just becoming warmed-up at 11.30 p.m. and there was no way they were going to let the disco stop. At 11.30 p.m. the Russians attempted to close it and everyone began stamping their feet. Realizing they were beaten, the Russian DJ put on some more records and tried to stop it again at 11.45 p.m. The same happened again, this time with more vigorous foot stamping, and they allowed it to continue until 12.00 a.m. But at midnight, in true Cinderella fashion, the Russians had had enough. Now everyone in the hall, and there must have been about 2000 of them, began stamping their feet like crazy and a few climbed onto the stage and started stamping with the result that some of the light bulbs got smashed. No sooner had this happened than the Soviet Army moved in. Armed soldiers swarmed in through every door and started to throw out the trouble-makers; and the only place left to go was to bed. Needless to say spirits were too high and too much alcohol had been consumed for that to happen and some behaved stupidly. Two of our swimmers were sent home in disgrace for drunkenly bursting into the rooms of some of the boxing team. It was a selfish thing to do because the boxers still had to compete and they needed their sleep. The swimmers had to be punished and the only punishment available was to send them home. Of course it was no hardship at all; more of a reward. We were all going home anyway within a day or two but the Russians wanted to show their displeasure so the offenders had to be put on the first available aeroplane home.

Indeed the Russians were visibly fuming about the bad behaviour. They were incapable, for instance, of seeing the humorous side of people festooned with spaghetti and chocolate cake in the dining halls and they were out for blood. My team would never have played these pranks if they had been given something that allowed them to work off their excess energy harmlessly but the Russians don't understand. For them it was all application, dedication and discipline but no, absolutely no, fun.

I was not involved in any of these antics. I used to see Michael, my Swedish boyfriend. I just used to like walking around the village with Michael and, though I heard all the rumpus going on, I was well away from it. I think I was the only swimmer who wasn't involved but then I was probably also the only one with a foreign boyfriend there.

The day after our two rioters had left with their tails between their legs we were leaving ourselves and it was not a moment too soon. The longer we were there the more trouble we would have caused and the more annoyed the Russians would have become. We all found the Soviet Union depressing and all of us wanted nothing more than to go home. The job had been done. The team had done well, I had my medal and all the hopes and dreams I had ever had were now a reality. I didn't realize it on that flight home but the next problem was to be even harder than any I had faced so far. What was I to do now?

CHAPTER EIGHT

Journalism and Judo

At Heathrow the press were out in force but the only people I wanted to see were my parents. Dad had flown back earlier and Mum had travelled up from Plymouth to form a welcoming committee and I just wanted to be with them and talk endlessly about all my Moscow experiences. I had not given a thought to my future but I knew I wasn't going to be doing any swimming for a while. It was time for a holiday. The pressure was off and I could now take time to consider my next move. As a wonderful bonus Michael came over to stay (originally for a week but, with the aid of some powder and a friendly doctor, a la Toronto, we had his flight ticket extended another week) and we just drove around the countryside, walked on the moors and played with Sam. It was a marvellous fortnight. For the first time that I could remember I was able to relax without the pressures of work hanging over me. I didn't go near a swimming pool and the last thing on my mind was a weight. To all intents and purposes Michael and I became sightseers. We visited parts of Britain I had never been to before and, for that brief fortnight, I enjoyed some of the childhood I had missed by racing up and down swimming pools.

When it was over I drove Michael to London to catch his aeroplane. That made me feel quite depressed but the news waiting for me on my return to Plymouth enveloped me in misery. Sam had been run over and killed. He had helped me so much at the beginning of the year that I felt part of my medal was really his. I loved him very much and his death jolted me out of the holiday mood and back into harsh reality. Sam and I had a telepathic link. I could make him do things without speaking and he had eyes for me only. Every night he used to come into my room for ten minutes to say goodnight and then, without my saying a word, he would go off to his bed in the kitchen. I felt then that no human being could ever be as close to me as Sam and his departure left a great gap in my life.

After about a month's break I started swimming training again and, in December, went to the South of France to participate in a brand new competition. It was an indoor, short course, European Championship and this time, because it was a western country, the East German who had beaten me in Moscow was disqualified for her illegal breaststroke and I won a gold medal. After that victory and the Christmas celebrations that followed the question for me was not: 'what am I going to do next in the pool' but 'what am I going to do with my life.' I had finished with school, there was little else I could have done at Kelly anyway.

So, I could try to find a job in Plymouth but I was not keen on that as it would have meant training at Kelly where my father was still coach. One alternative was to move to London and try another coach, which is what I had half expected to do after the Games, or I could do what so many other athletes had done before me, David Wilkie and Duncan Goodhew to name just two, and go to an American University.

I was a little ambivalent about the idea because, though I quite liked the notion of being a student on a campus with such fantastic facilities as those of the American Universities, I wasn't particularly keen on going to live in the States. Still, I had to investigate the idea and my mother and I went out to California to see if we could find a suitable university.

First I tried the University of Southern California where the pool for the 1984 Olympics had just been built – obviously a large factor in its favour – and then I looked at Stamford and Berkeley because of their good reputations academically. One of the things I particularly wanted to avoid was passing a degree at a university that had excellent swimming facilities but where the qualification was not worth the paper it was printed on. There are many such universities in America and Stamford and Berkeley were not among them – hence my interest. I also had a quick look at UCLA because I wanted to include Media Studies in my academic course and UCLA, near Hollywood, had a media school.

Sportswoman of the Year for the second time with the Sportsman of the Year, Steve Ovett. Personally I think he looks great with a beard
Keystone Press Agency

After seeing them all, however, I opted for Berkeley. It had the highest academic reputation, a nice campus (San Francisco is, in my opinion, a great deal nicer than Los Angeles anyway) and the pool was good with a young squad quickly developing under a keen and knowledgeable female coach. It seemed to offer everything.

In all my mother and I stayed in the United States for three weeks looking at the universities, trying out the pools and trying to reach a decision. But it wasn't until we were back in Plymouth that Berkeley rose to the top of the heap. As I have said I wasn't enthusiastic about the idea but I wasn't violently opposed to it either and it seemed the logical extension of my career. I just accepted, without emotion, that Berkeley was where I would go next.

But hardly had this decision been made than I went to the Sportswriters Dinner in London (I had been voted their top Sportswoman of the Year for the second time) and there I met Judo Champion Neil Adams. I had met him a few times before, at Crystal Palace and around the Olympic village, and I liked him but I was going out with Michael at the time and I didn't know Neil well. But at that Sportswriters Dinner we talked and talked; in fact I think we may even have fallen in love with each other then without realizing it.

At the dinner we talked about our respective careers and Neil suggested that, as I wanted to begin a career in the media, it would be more sensible to stay in London where the work was. It made good sense to me. I could take or leave university life and London was where I might be able to find journalistic work. It suddenly seemed logical to move to London and start gaining whatever practical experience I could.

It was good advice from Neil and I found him attractive so when, sometime during the dinner, he asked me to go to Coventry with him I agreed. I left a note for Mum and Dad, hid my trophy somewhere safe, and went with Neil that night. He had to make a speech at a school the following morning and we called in to see his mother on the way. She came to the door with her hair in rollers and asked who he had with him. When he replied, 'Sharron Davies', poor Mrs Adams rushed upstairs and didn't come down for what seemed like ages while she made herself look respectable. She was funny and I liked her and Neil's father, Cyril, very much.

Neil and I naturally started seeing each other quite often and it was not long before I made a definite decision to forget about California and concentrate on London. The United States seemed so big and impersonal, Neil wouldn't be there and Britain was my home, so here, I decided, I must stay. I had had the offer of some television work which had helped me to make up my mind but the main reason for staying in Britain, apart from Neil, was that my parents were finally splitting up and I felt I couldn't leave my mother completely alone. She and my brothers needed me and I felt I owed them whatever help I was able to give.

But though I travelled down to see them often, I still had to live in London because that was where the work was. I now had an agent who was finding me various bits and pieces of television work and I had to be in London to be in a position to accept them. So I packed all my bags and moved into a London hotel while I looked for a flat. No sooner had I arrived in the city than I had my car broken into and all my gear taken. Clothing, in fact all I possessed, worth £3000 in replacement value, was stolen and I was like a little girl lost in a big city with no clothes and no money. I was terribly upset anyway because of my parents and now I was an instant waif. I didn't know what to do. I had no insurance cover and no way of paying the hotel bill; it was a desperate situation. Of course I was not without friends and the practicalities were sorted out reasonably quickly but I still had few clothes, I still had to make my own way and my parents were still tugging at my loyalties.

Although I had known that my parents were far from happy for some time I was not aware that my father was seeing anyone else until after the Olympic Games. My mother hadn't known either until she discovered a letter from Alison to my father and she came to me for sympathy. She was definitely the injured party in the affair and she so obviously needed my support that I couldn't help taking her side. Dad had spent a great deal of money travelling up and down the country to see his girlfriend in secret. It seemed like treachery to me and the fact that Alison, his girlfriend, was only a year older than me made the whole situation seem even worse. Dad had spent the past ten years of his life wrapped up in my swimming and all the accompanying problems and he lived, nearly as much as me, on the adrenalin diet that goes with competition. It must have been hard on him when the special relationship we had had was over and he must have felt almost desolate but I couldn't find it in my heart to condone his deceit and it appalled me that he was actually living with someone of my own age.

Of course it was excellent meat for the press and they made a meal of it; exaggerating grossly, as usual. I did not say, for instance, that I was never going to speak to my father again. I said that he was a hard taskmaster, which he was, and I said he was often harder on me than he needed to be. I also said I found his new relationship hard to accept and didn't approve of the way he had treated my mother but I added that I felt it was a private affair and nothing to do with Fleet Street. It was too juicy a story for them to leave alone and an easy one for them to overstate.

As it turned out, I didn't speak to my father for a long time. He had behaved wrongly and treated my mother unfairly. Even when he was still living with her he had settled Alison into a flat just down the road and was seeing her every evening. I had felt that, as the marriage was so strained, they should leave one another but my father seemed to be drawing it out and causing far too much pain. A clean break would have been much kinder.

The papers, of course, said that I was so angry I had ended our coaching relationship. That was rubbish. It had ended because of the necessity for me to find a job and live in London. His work was at Kelly and mine was in London. There was no way we could have continued our sporting partnership several hundred miles apart. The press, however, drew the conclusions that they wanted – not for the first time – and, as usual, the truth was distorted. I am not saying, however, that if I had decided to stay in Plymouth Dad would have been my coach; he may not have been. But the simple truth was that I had no future at Kelly, had had enough of Plymouth and, to some degree, with swimming also. My future lay elsewhere. I certainly hadn't run to London to escape from Dad. The suggestion was so absurd it was laughable.

In the process of establishing a career in television I did try to start swimming under another coach but it didn't work. I was getting nowhere and I had lost much of my appetite for swimming anyway so I decided to forget swimming for a while and concentrate on my career.

During this time my father was having problems at Kelly. The school was distressed by the amount of scandal in the newspapers and the local papers were full of his nightly dashes between home and Alison's flat. It proved too much for the school and before too long they asked for his resignation. It didn't all happen immediately. The whole sordid episode dragged on for some time but eventually my father did resign, collected Alison and what was due to him, and moved to London to seek a new post. In all it took about a year. It was near Christmas 1981 when I heard he was coming to London. He had accepted a position as chief coach of Southwark Borough and he and Alison set up house together. Matters were, at last, beginning to sort themselves out.

My life was also taking a turn for the better. I had found myself a flat in Crystal Palace. My agent had secured me a job as a presenter on the ITV children's programme *Ace Reports* and I was on my way. Perhaps it wasn't the best programme to start on and I was completely out of my depth and didn't know what to do. In many ways, of course, that is the best way to learn but I felt that the programme had too many chiefs and not enough Indians. The programme format wasn't quite right and the directors didn't know whether they were coming or going. On my very first day on the programme I had to do a piece straight to camera. It was the first time I had ever done such a thing and I was neither given a run through nor any advice. Needless to say I wasn't very good but I did improve as the programme went on and I taught myself most of the television basics. At first I didn't even understand the jargon so I had no idea of what they were talking about. It was hard going but I persevered because I had to make a living. I was on my own with no money and no experience. My swimming success had helped me land the television work and I had to make every effort to make the maximum of the advantages I had. I knew that it was a chance that most people would never have and I was grateful but it was hard, hard work and there was no time left for swimming while I was coming to grips with it.

The press, naturally, were speculating that I had thrown swimming aside for the glitter of television but it wasn't strictly

Beginning my television career: reading the script in the studio in 1981
Associated Newspapers

true. Okay so I was invited to make guest appearances here and there on various television programmes and I was doing bits and pieces of writing for magazines but I was trying only to establish some sort of career for the future. I hadn't forgotten swimming by any means and still had the Brisbane Commonwealth Games in the back of my mind but I had to find a livelihood first. It was not a handsome living by any standards and I wasn't living in the lap of luxury that some people obviously imagined. I earned about £200 a programme out of which I had to pay tax, rent, food and transport. There wasn't much left over at the end and I wasn't comfortable let alone rich. It was also an insecure life. *Ace Reports* was only a 12-week contract. I wasn't a full-time employee of Thames, and I had to rely on my agent to keep the work coming in.

I would add a word of advice here, particularly to those sports-people who turn to the media for a living after they retire. It is a natural progression and they would be foolish not to capitalize on the fact that they are still fresh in the public eye. But I would warn those who do, especially those from 'young' sports like swimming and gymnastics, to seek independent and specialist advice before signing a contract with anyone. There is always someone ready to take advantage of your naiveté and relieve you of some of your earnings.

I found myself in a very unsatisfactory position at one stage because I signed a five-year exclusive contract with one agent. He became too busy to always find me adequate work and it led to many problems. We have negotiated a better arrangement now whereby if he finds me suitable work I am happy to do it and pay him his 20 per cent commission. But if someone else finds me work, I am free to accept that as well. In other words he is an unofficial agent along with several others. No one acts for me exclusively and I am at liberty to pick and choose whatever I want and whatever suits me best. If people phone me and the job is right I will do it. It is as simple as that.

I can do it quite successfully now because I understand how the system works. Athletes just coming into it would not have that knowledge. I would recommend to anyone starting out in the media and showbiz world, especially if they have that extra amount of naiveté that comes from growing up outside London, is to find a solicitor first and to ask him to check every document you are asked to sign. Never sign a contract of more than one year's duration and never assume that what is being done is being done for your welfare – always check. Remember it is better to spend £50 on a solicitor than lose £5000.

Although I was embittered by my introduction into the commercial world I did not have a nervous breakdown because of it and one of the reasons for this was Neil. He was my backbone and he saw to it that I came out of it without any scars.

I had been going out regularly with Neil from the moment we had met at the Sportswriters Dinner. After I had moved to London we saw each other regularly and, before long, he asked if I would marry him. I said no. I wanted a career and, even though I loved Neil and wanted to keep the close relationship we had (the closest I had ever had), I felt an engagement would come in the way of it. Neil wanted more commitment from me than that and he left. I don't know if he was just trying to teach me a lesson but, if he was, it worked. Within a week I lost half-a-stone in weight and decided I desperately needed him. I rang him and we met again and became engaged immediately.

At first we made great and lavish plans for marriage but, when we came down to earth and were less lovelorn, our marriage plans were put aside. In every way other than having that little piece of legal paper we were married. We bought a house together and acquired three dogs and a washing machine – all the necessary ingredients for domestic happiness – but I always baulked at the idea of the permanence of marriage. It seemed rather pointless to me to get married and accept all its responsibilities unless I was ready to have children and, though I still plan to have children and look forward to it, that time is still not yet here. Indeed I think that living with someone is the only way of discovering whether you want to marry them.

Even my parents approved of the arrangement. They realized that, partly because of the unorthodox nature of our jobs, we needed to learn about each other before making any decisions. Neil is still a practising sportsman wracked by its accompanying pressures. He

Someone who will always be very special to me. Neil Adams and I
trying our hand at windsurfing in 1981
Keystone Press Agency

was World Champion in his weight at Judo and he had the extra pressure that comes with staying at the top – psychologically a considerably greater strain than chasing someone for a title. Because I had felt most of these pressures myself I was able to provide a shoulder and a support but it wasn't easy at times. Neil was still deep in training, with all the lonely fitness work that that entails, and I was moving in the more glamorous world of the media and public relations. In my business being young and unattached was a positive advantage and Neil found that hard to accept. He was very jealous which I found increasingly difficult to deal with. He used to have fits of anger that really had to be seen to be believed. He could not understand that my job was to talk to other people and that I had to be convincing at it. Neil, perhaps through insecurity, felt there was more to it. He didn't understand I could do the sort of work that I did without exploiting my female charms.

The problem was that Neil had a different way of venting his anger from me and my father, for instance. Instead of having several minor eruptions a day Neil would bottle things up until he could contain them no longer and then he would blow the whole world apart. He has thrown a kettle through the kitchen window and put his fist through the walls but he never struck out at me. I learnt to be somewhere else when Neil hit the roof – I used to treat it rather like the weather and ride it out.

However, after three and a half years, we finally decided to part. Somehow, probably because the demands of our careers have not changed, we seemed unable to overcome our problems. We still love each other very much and remain the best of friends but, for the present at least, we seem to be better apart.

What was more difficult at the time was ignoring the comments in the press and by people in swimming. Everyone said I had given it up for the glamour. It just wasn't true and it annoyed me that people believed these lies. I was taking a much-needed break; everyone seemed to forget that I had been swimming for ten years and had been competing at top-class level since I was eleven. Quite simply I was stale. I was not enjoying swimming any more and I needed time off to recharge my batteries. I also had to find some way of earning a living and that didn't leave much time for training. The job occupied the whole day and left no time for swimming. If I was to train as hard as I needed in order to take up where I had left off I would have had to give up the job altogether, and I just could not afford to do that. Besides I didn't have a coach to train with anyway and it seemed sensible to use this period to find my feet and become settled, and then go back to swimming when I was fresh and keen for success again.

It was not as if I was not keeping fit or putting on weight. I still did weight circuits three times a week and in the ten months or so that I had off I actually lost half-a-stone. It was a time of reassessment and replenishment for me. The ten years spent constantly worrying about who could reach the end of a swimming pool first had taken their toll and I needed to discover myself as a person before I thought of taking to the water again.

When that time did come I was hungry to win . . . but others were equally keen that I did not have the opportunity.

CHAPTER NINE

Brisbane Ruled Out

The Commonwealth Games were always my favourite meet. I had had a wonderful time at Edmonton and the thought of going to such friendly games again, with the added advantage of four years' experience, was very attractive. I knew that if I started training seriously I could win and I began to think about returning to full-time training at about the same time as my father came to London to take up his post at Southwark. It seemed the logical step to train with him again.

There was still some conflict between us but my own relationship with Neil had helped me to see things in a much more adult way and I found I was able to, if not approve then at least to understand something of his point of view. When I had sided with Mum against Dad I hadn't been aware of the complexity of human relationships. I tended to look at the affair in black and white; but the years with Neil had opened my eyes and I could see, for the first time, why my father had behaved as he had. I could see, for instance, that he kept trying to hang on to his marriage because part of him was hoping that his love for Alison would disappear. He didn't want to destroy his marriage in case the situation at home changed – and it may have changed because they both knew the time was coming when I would be leaving home. My mother hoped that when my swimming was over he would settle down again and resume the ordinary life they had had before the swimming started. I think my father may have had that thought too at the back of his mind and, though he loved Alison, he didn't want to commit himself, one way or the other, until he was absolutely certain.

Eventually, of course, final decision time arrived and he chose to start a new life for himself with Alison in London. They found themselves a flat in Camberwell and he threw himself into his job with the Southwark pools. Since then they have experienced the ups and downs of any normal couple but, on the whole, they have been very happy. They were married in November 1983 and had a baby daughter, Lissa, at the beginning of 1984 whom I adore.

My mother had more difficulty in starting a new life for herself but she has found her feet again now and she has met someone else. She knows again that there is more to life than being miserable. She has cut her hair, lost weight and she looks more like my sister than my mother. It made me very happy when I saw this change taking place because I had worried about her perhaps more than she realized. I was aware that she still had life ahead of her to enjoy but I couldn't say so because she was in such despair. Now she knows how to make the most of what she has and she is far happier for it. It is not all happy families again in the Davies clan by any means but things are looking up and the worst of the business has subsided.

Of course, all this took some time to come about but it started as soon as my father came to London. We had a chat at the time and I told him I wanted to go to Brisbane and that I would like him to coach me. Dad was enthusiastic about the idea and I slipped back into the pool almost as though I had never left it: and this time I could do it without any worries. I had established myself in a career – people accepted me as a television presenter – I was engaged and I had a home of my own; I was independent and secure, and I could put everything into my training safe in that knowledge.

It wasn't easy, of course. I didn't like getting up at five in the morning for training again and I was always tired when I came home in time to make breakfast and pull Neil out of bed. I couldn't stop then though, I still had to work and I still had to go to Southwark again in the evening for the second training session. The old form was returning and I wanted to go to Brisbane so much that I settled into the routine without complaint. But storm clouds were gathering.

When I submitted my times for entry in a local competition, they refused my entry. Naturally I asked why and the reply was a feeble 'We don't know what the ASA will say.' It was absurd. If they had just accepted the entry the ASA would not have interfered but now,

Tired but happy after putting up the qualifying time for the Brisbane
Commonwealth Games at Crystal Palace in July 1982
Associated Newspapers

when we went ourselves to the ASA to ask for the ruling to be changed, the governing body also refused to allow me to swim. They also declined to give me a reason and my father and I felt we had no option but to take them to court.

Even with this threat hanging over them they still didn't provide a reason for barring me. They did not appear in Court to present their case and the judge granted me a 24-hour injunction to allow me to swim in the competition and record, if I was able, the qualifying time for the Games.

So, once again, I found myself the centre of attention in the sporting press. There were reporters lurking around every corner and it wasn't uncommon for my telephone to ring at three in the morning as some reporter sought a last quote for his copy. In the main they seemed to be on my side and I didn't object to them doing their work as I thought it may have the effect of pressurizing the ASA into changing its position.

The day before the competition for which I had the injunction I went out riding, fell off and compressed the bottom three vertebrae of my spine. I could hardly stand up let alone swim but I had no choice. I had the injunction for the day only and I had to put up the qualifying time or face the possibility of not going to Brisbane at all. So when it was time to swim I was taking painkillers. This was strictly illegal and had I been dope tested my time would not have stood but what could I do? It was either take paninkillers or not swim at all and I had to give myself whatever chance I could. Besides it wasn't as if painkillers speed you up, if anything they do the opposite.

When the time came to swim I found that I was not to be allowed to swim with the others. The organizers were quite pleasant but they insisted that, if I wanted to swim I would have to do so by myself. I felt as if I had a contagious disease but I swam on my own and managed the qualifying time easily. I have to say that all the other swimmers were marvellous. They stood around the pool and cheered like crazy. They didn't agree with the ridiculous stand the ASA was taking and they wanted to give me all the support they could. Their gesture made me feel that at least someone was on my side and it made me more determined than ever to put up a good time and to fight for my rights.

With my father at Crystal Palace in July 1982
Sport and General

The officials' viewpoint, however, was very weak-minded. They said that, if the ASA ruled me professional I would be banned from competing and that, therefore, the other swimmers could not be allowed in the same pool with me. It did not occur to them that, even if I was declared professional, the ruling would take effect only from the time of the hearing. Until that time I was an amateur and fit to swim in any of their competitions. Their decision was small-minded and petty and was an example of the eagerness of the ASA to exert its authority. They were being unreasonable and I was totally convinced that I was in the right.

My plan was to go back to court to force the ASA to stand down but I had a meeting with them and they said that that would be pointless. Their view was that such a course would cost everyone a great deal of money and they suggested that we settle out of court at a hearing of the ASA's Southern Counties. I agreed and, with my solicitor, prepared my case; but it was to no avail.

The Swimming Association's case was founded on the fact that my name was written on the back of my car – which it was. However, just having your name on a car was not against the rules as long as it was not for gain and I was definitely receiving no payment for it. The car had not been given to me and it was no perk – I was paying for it by hire purchase and it was for my personal use only. We showed them all the legal documentation relating to the car – proving that no profit was made from it.

But they were not beaten. Their next step was to suggest that I had accepted a fee of £40 for appearing on a TV programme called *Give Us A Clue*. I had appeared on this programme and it was all very innocent but the trouble was that I had been introduced as Sharron Davies, Olympic swimmer as well as Sharron Davies, TV presenter. *Give Us A Clue* was a guessing game programme and most of the guest panellists were actors and actresses – not sportspeople. I thought I had been invited on it because of my TV work and because I had made a short film which had been quite well received. I had also presented a whole children's series and I was as well known for this type of work as some of the other guests. In other words appearing on that programme was a natural sidestep to my work as a TV personality. It had nothing to do with my being a swimmer, I was simply pursuing my journalistic work.

As far as I could see, I had broken none of the amateur rules but they thought that, by accepting the £40 fee (which could so easily have been written off as legitimate expenses), I had acted as a professional. I realized the intransigence of their attitude so I asked them to accept that, if the rules had been broken, they had been broken in ignorance. I think I even offered to atone for my 'mistake' by paying the £40 to a charity. But they wouldn't hear of it.

As far as they were concerned I had used my reputation as a swimmer to find me work I would not otherwise have been given. It was unfair. If I had decided to join a bank, for instance, the bank may have employed me partly because I was Sharron Davies – not necessarily because I was the best girl for the job. It would have been good publicity to have me on the staff and it would have been the same with any employer. No matter what I decided to do I would always be given some form of preference simply because many people had heard of me. Thus, by the ASA argument, I would have been using my swimming fame for personal gain and therefore a professional. I am certain that if I had chosen bank work for my career they would have found that perfectly acceptable but, because my job placed me in the public eye and attracted some publicity which had nothing to do with swimming, they refused to compromise and remained resolute.

It was so frustrating. I was engaged in a profession that I had decided on, years before, while still at Plymstock Comprehensive. I was not just an opportunist on the media bandwagon, I had genuinely planned to work in the field for many years and now I was being punished for making my living from the type of work that interested me most.

Irrespective of any argument from my solicitor and me, the ASA stood their ground and declared me a professional. In doing so, however, they said that I could apply for reinstatement on the grounds that my professionalism was accidental rather than deliberate. I was very upset but I accepted this because I thought it was a way out. I thought that, because I had won in court and they had appeared in an unfavourable light, they wanted to make their point at the hearing and then accept me back quietly afterwards. It seemed to me as if any other course would be equally damaging to them. I was one of their best swimmers and one of their better medal prospects for Brisbane and I couldn't believe that they would not reinstate me when I went on bended knees and begged forgiveness.

It would certainly have been in their interests to accept me back. I would win medals for them and attract the sort of press coverage that could only be beneficial. In my ten years as a competitive swimmer I had never done swimming any harm. I wasn't asking for trust funds or any special privileges . . . all I wanted was a chance to swim for Britain and the opportunity to earn my own living. I was sure that, when they reconsidered it, they would see the sense of it and allow me to go to Brisbane with the team. Not once had I written, talked or been paid for anything to do with swimming. I was not a professional and I felt sure that they too would realize this before long.

But time was slipping by. I didn't recognize it then but it was all part of the ASA's overall plan. If they said a decision would be reached in two weeks it took four. All this time I was continuing to train and lose income but I couldn't believe that I would be barred from swimming. When the reinstatement hearing took place I was certain they would reinstate me but I had been present a few minutes only when they turned around and pronounced 'no'.

It was like a kick in the teeth and I could hardly believe it: it was as though I was being punished for something more than just *Give Us A Clue*. I knew that the only way their decision could be reversed was by recourse to the courts. It would cost me a small fortune but I was still a swimmer and I wanted badly to swim in Brisbane. It had already cost me £3500 just to obtain a High Court injunction and I couldn't see myself embarking on more protracted litigation without spending £10,000. Even so I went ahead and set proceedings in motion.

Again, perhaps naively, I thought my chances were reasonable. The reinstatement vote had gone only four to three against me and I knew I had some allies within the Association. I felt that by going through the motions of the legal system again, these allies would rise and save the day.

When I went back to my solicitor and said I had decided to go back to court, he supported me. He knew that they could not prove I had broken any of the amateur rules as defined in the amateur rule book and he believed that, if it was left to the Law, I would be swimming for England again within a short space of time.

But the ASA's dawdling paid dividends for them. Although my solicitor had said I had the best possible case, he also told me that the courts were in summer recess. It would be impossible for me to take up the case again before about 15 November. It was the last cruel straw that broke my back. The Commonwealth Games themselves were in September and, if I couldn't go to Court until after the Games, there was no point in going to Court at all. They had beaten me, quite simply, through wasting time. I am certain it was deliberate on their part just as I am certain that it was a powerful faction within the ASA which, for reasons that completely elude me, had decided Sharron Davies would never again swim for Britain. No one gave any thought to the fact that I had brought some prestige to British women's swimming. No one concerned themselves with the fact that, at 19, I had devoted more than half my life to the sport, and it never occurred to anyone that I deserved some consideration for the efforts I had made on behalf of their sport. My anonymous enemies had beaten me, and I found myself expelled, ignominiously, with no effective course of redress. I didn't know the reason but I felt cheated and unwanted and I couldn't understand it.

In retrospect, I realize that I probably couldn't have gone back to Court anyway. I would have liked to and I would have tried to raise the money but, unless someone had helped me, there was no way I could possibly have found the funds. At the time I was deadly serious and I would have tried to raise it no matter what but, being realistic, my chances alternated between slim and no chance at all.

It was so frustrating; unbelievably frustrating. I was the Commonwealth record holder for both of my main events and I was the only team member to bring back a gold from the previous Commonwealth Games. Why were they seemingly acting against their own reason, namely winning swimming competitions? I didn't know the answer then and I still do not know it today. It is totally incomprehensible to me; the ASA surely could not have actually wanted to come back from Brisbane with less medals than the country could have won, could they?

Some people suggested to me that the ASA were frightened that, if they allowed me to swim, they would open the flood gates and lose control. Those who had broken the amateur rules would have grounds to force their way back into the sport. I did not take the argument seriously.

Despite the controversy, the ASA did not use it as an opportunity to look at the system to see why this situation had arisen. To reach the top in swimming now, as with every other sport, the athlete needs to give up so much that there is no time left to earn a livelihood, unless a sponsor is forthcoming. Just in order to continue, athletes are increasingly being forced to accept under-the-table deals and yet some of the sports bodies refuse to study this ever-changing situation and create conditions that will allow sportspeople to pursue their sports with the necessary dedication while receiving some financial remuneration for the sacrifices they have made on their sport's behalf.

The rules relating to sponsors are responsible for keeping a great deal of money that could be invested in swimming out of the sport. When my father negotiated a sponsorship deal with Wimpey Construction he was not allowed to arrange it for me and a coach only. The rules compelled him to organize a package to include a whole squad of some 40 Kelly swimmers. In that particular case we were lucky and Wimpey agreed despite the fact that initially they had intended to sponsor a small group only. It costs a fantastic amount of money to maintain a full squad and Wimpey would far rather have just put their backing behind an elite team. Wimpey put in the extra sponsorship and many swimmers who otherwise would not have had the benefits of a sponsor received it; but there are lots of other firms and individuals who, though they would like to put their money behind a 'name' cannot shoulder the increased burden of a whole squad.

Other sports have found ways out of this dilemma and it is long overdue for swimming to bring itself up-to-date and find ways of allowing people who dedicate their lives to the sport to receive some financial recognition.

Philip Hubble, for instance, who is one of the very best swimmers Britain has produced, and one of the hardest workers for the sport, was refused permission to accept an offer of sponsorship. It has meant that, in order to find the training that he needs, he has had to go back to the United States. He doesn't want to live and train there – he would far rather live and work in Britain – but the ostriches of swimming administration refuse to remove their heads from the sand. Effectively they are undermining our sport, not providing a service, and they should alter their thinking before Britain loses the good team it has at the moment and slides, once again, into the backwaters of the sport. It is already happening before their very eyes and they could reverse it so easily if only they would see the practicalities of the situation.

They will not listen to the swimmers and they will not listen to the press. Throughout the whole of my battle for amateur status the press were unbelievably on my side. At the time whenever I walked out into the street at least 20 people – members of the public as well as journalists – would come up to wish me luck and say they really hoped I would swim. Almost every day one of the papers expressed criticism of the stand the ASA was taking but the ASA remained staunchly silent and refused to be drawn. They couldn't adequately justify their action so they resorted to silence.

From that time until the present day I have heard not a single word from the Association. They ended my career and then conveniently forgot my existence. Of course they can't completely forget me because most of my records still stand and some may well stand for a long time but they have been responsible for preventing me from culling the fruits of my labours. Neil, for instance, has an MBE for his services to judo and Daley, who was passed over after Moscow because the Government was not keen to reward the athletes who went to the Soviet Union, eventually was given one for his work in sport. I was once told that an MBE would be forthcoming for me and it would have been a great honour.

It is a minor point but it's also a sign of recognition of one's contribution to a sport. Naturally, I would have liked to have been honoured with an MBE. I gave my sport everything I had. I believe I deserved one and for the ASA to deny it to me (and it is the ASA that makes the nominations to the Government) seems unfair.

Before all this happened I had never had any reason to disagree with the ASA. I hadn't been known for misbehaving and I had always done whatever was asked of me in the pool. In fact, I had often been chosen as captain of the women's team. To be humiliated like this at the end of my career (the Commonwealth Games would have been my last major event anyway), seemed a great pity. They hurt me, but far worse is that they are damaging my sport; and for that I will never forgive them.

CHAPTER TEN

A New Career

Despite the fact that I am basically a very sensible person, not given to over-reaction, I took that ASA decision very hard. For about a month afterwards I wallowed in a sea of anxiety and depression and I found it difficult to concentrate on anything else. I couldn't train any more, there seemed little point anyway, and I found it difficult to focus on my work and I had to turn down several opportunities just because I felt too depressed.

But before too long the Davies pragmatism bubbled to the surface and I became determined to start something new: to make a new life for myself. I was not yet sure what it was going to be but I was adamant that it should be something that I could develop as a new career. I was going to be just as successful as I was before.

Following the decision to ban me from competing I had dozens of offers to do promotional work. My battle with the ASA had been 'hot news' and now some companies wanted me to exploit my notoriety by endorsing their products. I received offers from television and newspapers asked me to write sensational stories exposing the behind-the-scenes world of swimming. Indeed there were plenty of opportunities to make some money. One men's magazine, I can't remember which one now, offered me about £10,000 to strip off and do a photo session. I was short of money at the time and it was almost tempting but, when I really thought about it, there were no circumstances under which I would do such work. I used to feel terribly embarrassed just standing around in swimming costumes and I have spent my life doing that – the thought of taking all my clothes off and posing was just too terrifying.

I have done one television advertisement with Duncan Goodhew which looks as if I was topless but I swear I wasn't. I spent a whole day shooting the swimming sequence and then the second was to be spent filming in the shower. When I arrived the producer asked me if I minded going topless to which I replied I did. Immediately men appeared from every nook and cranny. There were about six sound men and six cameramen . . . they seemed to come from everywhere. How they thought I was going to undress in front of all of them I'll never know. The producer, of course, tried to persuade me to change my mind with such comments as everyone else did it, why not me. I replied that I wasn't everyone else – I was Sharron Davies and I didn't do topless shots. Impasse.

After much debate a piece of cloth and some sellotape was produced and this was taped around my bust and the shower filming begun. Soon, however, the piece of cloth became wet and when it did it became see-through. We were in the middle of a shot when I noticed it and I stopped proceedings straight away, covering myself up with my arms and demanding that they thought again about a way of covering me up. Finally some bright spark came up with a packet of plasters and I went off to the lavatory to stick these all over. It was agony taking them off later but it was well worth it because they worked perfectly. They were skin coloured so it looked as though I was having my shower in the nude but in fact I was covered in so many plasters I would have been considered overdressed in some places.

As I have already said I was receiving plenty of opportunities to endorse products and I did lend my name to many companies but I knew that I would not remain a 'name' for ever and would have to find some other field, sooner or later, in which I excelled. There wasn't anyone coming up in women's swimming so fast that they were going to knock me from my perch but I had been in the media long enough to realize its fickleness. The stars of today are all too often forgotten by tomorrow and I was determined not to let that happen to me.

I had already decided that a career as a television presenter was not really for me. I liked some of the programmes that I did, especially the ones that allowed me to be myself, but most of the time I was reciting prepared speeches and I was not satisfied. I knew that I had to find something else.

I needed a career that others would respect and in which I had some say. I had never been one to stay in the background and, like my father, I had never been one to be told what to do or suffer fools gladly. If I was going to be successful and happy I had to be my own boss and I had to find a business which would use my talents fully. I knew I liked fashion and I thought I understood better than most the special demands that sportspeople require in leotards, costumes and tracksuits. I was sure that I knew enough to survive in the world of fashion and I was sufficiently fashion conscious to be able to marry the whims of fashion with the practical necessities of training wear.

The problem was getting into the business but I knew there was a big gap in the market for a high-quality British product. What sportspeople needed was gear that could stand up to the hardest wear but still be smart and casual enough to wear every day. I had ideas for just the thing in my head; but how to put those ideas into practice?

I mentioned this problem to my accountant and he fortunately was able to introduce me to a couple of businessmen keen to enter the same field. He arranged a meeting and the idea grew until we set up the company ESDE (the SD for Sharron Davies), with the three of us as co-directors. I didn't put up any cash to set up the company – I didn't have any – but I did a great deal of work. My main work lay in using my name to promote the product but I also became heavily involved with the design. I knew exactly what I wanted but I didn't have the proper designing and cutting skills needed so I worked with a professional and together we developed my ideas into a finished product. It took a year before our whole range was prepared and it was hard work but when it was finished I was proud of it and proud to have my name associated with it. It made the job of endorsement easy because I knew from first-hand that it was a quality product that lives up to its claims.

I would not have succeeded on my own and both my partners were very experienced businessmen so I was able to leave much of that side to them. They organized a very professional launch at Stringfellows and they arranged that our line was accepted by Lillywhites, Harrods, D. H. Evans, Miss B. and many other first-class shops.

Not to be modest, we have done quite well. We are a go-ahead company, always looking for ways to expand and ways to extend the range. I enjoy the commercial world and would love to be successful in my own right as a businesswoman. From the beginning I wanted to be involved as closely as I could with all aspects of the company and I played a part in everything except production. Even in that area, however, I am a sort of trouble shooter. When we produce a garment I road test it and if I think it shrinks too much or is made of insufficient quality material I tell them to put it right. They know I will not allow my name to be associated with a shoddy product and the end result is satisfaction all round; certainly I have great hopes for the future.

But I didn't devote all my time to ESDE. I was sufficiently experienced now and had been burned too many times to do that. If and when ESDE expands I will undoubtedly want to spend far more time working for it but, at the moment, I spread my activities over as wide an area as possible. I have to keep myself in the public eye – as a source of income and as a source of publicity for ESDE – and I am involved in other business ventures. I do quite a lot of television work (and, if all goes well, even more in the future), and I have even dabbled in the film world and made a few health videos.

Not long after my enforced swimming retirement I was asked to play the lead role in a half-hour silent comedy film for Channel 4. I agreed immediately and enjoyed it tremendously. We had to go to Mexico for the filming which was exciting but I found the country itself depressing. We stayed in a luxury hotel with marble fountains while just around the corner was the worst poverty I had ever seen. The difference between rich and poor was appalling and I didn't like being pampered when so many others were literally dying from hunger nearby. I was also taken aback by the filth of the place. For instance, a dead horse was left lying in the middle of the square. No one came to take it away – no one even covered it – people simply walked around it as though it wasn't there.

The film was a simple triangle comedy. I played a windsurfer girl chased by two boys and a series of slapstick situations ensued. It was the first filming I had done and I found it fascinating and I would do it again if the right part came along but I don't think I

Modelling ESDE sportswear

would find it preferable to my interest in business; that is really my top priority and prime goal at the moment.

I have had offers for other film work, however. After this film was shown on Channel 4, I was asked to audition for *Supergirl* – a female version of *Superman* – but when I went to the audition realized that they wanted someone who was five foot seven and five foot eleven was just a bit too tall! If an interesting film did come along and the producer wanted me to do it I would probably agree. It is, after all, good fun, well paid and excellent publicity. But it would have to be a good film and I am not interested in chasing work in the film industry. If it happens, fine, but at the moment I am quite happy as I am now. I am not at all sure that I would like the lifestyle. There's the added disadvantage, too, that people who work hard in films are not necessarily the ones who make the most money. I would far rather spend my life doing something that rewarded me in direct proportion to the amount of work I was putting in. I'd rather work terribly hard in a business and succeed than try to survive in the world of celluloid where it is often more a case of who you know.

As well as ESDE I am involved in another company based in Plymouth that gives advice on all aspects of health club organization. The company will undertake all aspects from building clubs to designing the wall decoration. Everything to do with health and fitness is in the overall brief of the company. Gym owner Garry Richards, who helped me so much during my year at Kelly, is a member of the team which advises anyone on fitness, gym equipment, saunas . . . you name it we cover it. As well as Garry there are specialists in various aspects of interior decorating and design on the team as well as Neil and myself. We are all experienced in this field and devoted to fitness. It is something that I know about and where I think I can help others who want to get the most from their gym or fitness work. Neil and I have made a sports video together for this reason.

Fitness generally is a growth business but there are far too many people who fall by the wayside. Garry, Neil and I are in a position to supply advice and also help to raise the standards of the clubs themselves.

The company is also involved in the development of home gyms (the Family Fit-Kit) and Neil and I hope to market one in the not too distant future. It is a piece of gym equipment that uses hydraulics rather than weights and is capable of supplying a wide range of exercises. It is equivalent to about 0–150 lbs of old-fashioned weights but it is light and easy to carry and store. We are hoping that it will be successful but we still have a long way to go. As with the ESDE clothing I tested the prototype when it was built and put it through all its paces. It was very satisfactory and we are keeping our fingers crossed that we can market it in the United States quite soon.

It's not going to make us rich overnight, however. We will not be able to promote it in the way we think it deserves and any profits we make will immediately be ploughed back into the business.

What promotional capacity we do have I intend to use in the United States where I am keen to also market the idea of professional fitness as undertaken by a British athlete. It is a novel idea that I hope will work. I think it is also important that we sell fitness as an organized professional activity – not as a pastime that happens in church halls and is led by unqualified people. I am keen on dance exercises, I don't like the word aerobics – it just gives a scientific name to an activity being practised by dedicated but unqualified amateurs in the main – and I would like to include that in my American programme. Aerobics, as commonly practised, can be very unsafe. Most of the classes are too big, the teacher is not sufficiently qualified, she can't see the person at the back of the room and she has too wide a range of ability in the class which leads to some being pushed too hard and others not enough. With 'Movement to Music', we would overcome all of these problems.

Although I very rarely swim now – I'm too busy and live too far from a pool to be able to fit it into my day – I haven't altogether given up the water. Another of my plans, this time in association with Duncan Goodhew, is to set up an 'Exercising in Water' pro-gramme. It will not appeal to as many people as exercising in gyms but it is excellent for people with joint problems and the like and would be a boon for those who cannot keep themselves fit, perhaps because of injury. Once in the water there is greatly reduced gravity and people with weight or joint problems can exercise much more safely than they could normally.

There is a possibility that Duncan and I may form a company to raise the finance for this programme but it is still very much at the planning stage. Duncan is very keen and he is one of my oldest friends from swimming and we have had some fun times together over the years. Now he is retired and battling to make a living in the same business as myself, we have even more in common. He doesn't live very far from me and I see him quite often – more frequently than any of the other swimmers I used to know – so it is almost inevitable that, sooner or later, we will work more closely together; and the water exercise scheme seems quite a good place to start.

Many people are quite shocked that I spend so little time now in a swimming pool. They feel that I squeezed all I could from it when I was in it and, now that it is no longer any use to me, have dropped it like a hot potato. In some ways, of course, this is true. It is an example of the old Davies trait of accepting reality, forgetting the past and concentrating on the present. I still like swimming, of course, and whenever I have a chance I will swim. I often coach when the opportunity arises and find I can work very well with swimmers. I am enthusiastic about the Olympics, of course, and I hope to be at the Los Angeles Games as a commentator for a TV network but that is the extent of any connection I have with swimming in the future.

Suffice it to say that competitive swimming is over for me. I know I can not revive it now. I will, of course, exploit my connection with swimming and the fame it brought me to the utmost; I would be foolish not to use my name to help me start off this all-important second phase of my life but I don't anticipate that I will need it for ever. It's a big challenge, far bigger than swimming itself, but it is not going to beat me. That isn't my way.